Entrepreneur
MAGAZINE'S

start*up*

Start Your Own

2ND EDITION

BUSINESS ON eBAY

*Your Step-by-Step
Guide to Success*

Entrepreneur Press and Jacquelyn Lynn

EP
Entrepreneur
Press

Additional titles in *Entrepreneur's* **Startup Series**

Start Your Own

Bed & Breakfast

Business on eBay

Business Support Service

Car Wash

Child Care Service

Cleaning Service

Clothing Store

Coin-Operated Laundry

Consulting

Crafts Business

e-Business

e-Learning Business

Event Planning Business

Executive Recruiting Service

Freight Brokerage Business

Gift Basket Service

Growing and Selling Herbs
  and Herbal Products

Home Inspection Service

Import/Export Business

Information Consultant Business

Law Practice

Lawn Care Business

Mail Order Business

Medical Claims Billing Service

Personal Concierge Service

Personal Training Business

Pet-Sitting Business

Restaurant and Five Other
  Food Businesses

Self-Publishing Business

Seminar Production Business

Specialty Travel & Tour Business

Staffing Service

Successful Retail Business

Vending Business

Wedding Consultant Business

Wholesale Distribution Business

Start Your Own

BUSINESS ON eBAY

Editorial Director: Jere L. Calmes
Managing Editor: Marla Markman
Cover Design: Beth Hansen-Winter
Production and Composition: studio Salt

This publication is designed to provide accurate and authoritative information in regard to the subject matter covered. It is sold with the understanding that the publisher is not engaged in rendering legal, accounting, or other professional services. If legal advice or other expert assistance is required, the services of a competent professional person should be sought.

Library of Congress Cataloging-in-Publication Data

Lynn, Jacquelyn.
   Start your own business on eBay/by Entrepreneur Press and Jacquelyn Lynn.–2nd ed.
     p.   cm.
   Rev. ed. of: Entrepreneur magazine's start your own business on eBay. 2004.
   ISBN-13: 978-1-59918-086-1 (alk. paper)
   ISBN-10: 1-59918-086-3 (alk. paper)
     1. Internet auctions. 2. eBay (Firm) 3. Electronic commerce–Management.
4. New business enterprises–Management. 5. Small business–Management. I. Lynn, Jacquelyn. Entrepreneur magazine's start your own business on eBay. II. Entrepreneur Press. III. Title.

HF5478.L96 2007
658.8'7–dc22   2007002462

Printed in United States

12 11 10 09 08 07   10 9 8 7 6 5 4 3 2

Contents

▲

▲

Preface

It's one of those business success stories that has already become a legend in its own time: eBay, the hottest way to buy and sell goods and services over the internet.

Online auctions in general and eBay in particular are changing the way merchandise is bought and sold all over the world. They've made it easier than ever for people to start retail businesses and for existing businesses to expand to a worldwide market.

When we say, "start an eBay business," what we really mean is to start a business that uses eBay as a marketing and distribution tool, or to add this element to an existing operation. You're not starting an "eBay business"; you're starting a business selling whatever products you've decided to sell on eBay. This book is not about how to start an online auction business; it's about how to use online auctions, eBay in particular, to start and grow your own business.

Are you a little uncomfortable with the idea of doing business in the vast world of cyberspace? Don't be. E-commerce is finally finding its place in the business world. The spectacular rise and equally spectacular crash of the dotcoms during the '90s was just part of the process of learning how to best use the internet. What happened in the dotcom debacle is not unique in business. It's happened in other industries at other points in history. People get excited and for some reason decide that the basic fundamentals of doing business don't apply to them. And they fail.

If you're excited about doing business on eBay, that's great. You should be. Just don't get so excited that you do stupid things. If you start to run your company using sound business principles, you'll succeed.

Keep in mind that many of the dotcom companies that were formed in the 1990s are still thriving. Why? Because they have products people want to buy, they have a clear plan, and they use sound business management techniques. If you choose your products carefully, develop a plan, and manage your operation well, your company will join the ranks of successful e-commerce operations. This book will help you do that, but it won't do the work for you, and it won't tell you how to make jillions of dollars working just two hours a week. What it will do is serve as a guide, a roadmap for you to use in getting your company launched. Like most businesses, operating on eBay will offer rewards proportionate to your efforts. With your own plan, a system, and the perseverance to follow it through, you can enjoy consistent profits from your eBay activities.

A lot of companies out there offer plans and systems to help people get started in an online business. Some are legitimate, but too many are scams that will just cost you money. And some of the legitimate operators sell the same advice to all their clients, which means you risk ending up with a cookie-cutter operation that has the same look and same products as hundreds of other sites, with lots of competition and few, if any, customers. Nothing can take the place of doing your own research and preparation, and putting the stamp of your own personality on your business.

Maybe, like many of the eBay sellers we talked with, you're a shopper who needs to make money to continue to buy. Or like one seller, you've bought too much and want to get rid of that stuff. Or like all the sellers we talked with, you have an entrepreneurial spirit, you want to start your own business, and eBay is an appropriate sales vehicle.

Whatever is motivating you, know this: Doing business on eBay is fun, exciting, profitable—and hard work. If you're not willing to put in the effort and the hours, no amount of information will make you successful.

Regardless of the particular type of business you want to own, how much money you have, whether you want to be homebased or operate from a commercial location, this book will tell you how to use eBay to start and grow. We'll begin with an overview of online auctions, look at the products and services you can sell, and then go through the step-by-step process of setting up and running your new venture. Throughout the book, you'll hear from successful eBay sellers who have built profitable operations and are eager to share what they've learned in the process. Of course, reading a book can only take you so far; once you actually start selling on eBay, you'll work and learn as you go.

Whether you plan to start a part-time business by yourself or jump into eBay selling full time and hire employees, we recommend you read every chapter in this book because most of the information applies to all sizes and types of eBay operations, and the information is interrelated.

So relax and start reading. The thrilling and lucrative world of selling on eBay is within your reach.

1

Introduction
to eBay

The goal of this book is to teach you how to build a profitable business selling on eBay—and the most important word in this sentence is *profitable*. Making sales on eBay is simple, and you can learn how to do that by just browsing the site. But if you're serious about your business, then the point of selling on eBay is to make a profit.

Beware!
eBay transactions are between the buyer and seller. As the online auction site, eBay is merely the vehicle that brings the buyer and seller together. eBay will assist with disputes but is not ultimately responsible for the transaction.

Before we get into the nuts and bolts of successful eBay selling, let's take a look at how this opportunity came to be.

The first online auction venue hit the internet in 1994. The following year, Pierre Omidyar introduced the site that would eventually be known as eBay. Originally called Auction Web, it started out as a kind of virtual garage sale, but with the added excitement of auction pricing. And it was so successful that it didn't take long for other online auction sites to pop up.

The big advantage of online auctions is that they expand a seller's market from a relatively small local group to essentially anyone with a computer and access to the internet. And it didn't take long for major companies, both business-to-consumer and business-to-business, to realize that this was a sales opportunity they couldn't afford to overlook.

What this means for you as an eBay seller is that you've stepped onto a level playing field that's populated with sellers that range from small part-timers who may not post even an auction a month to huge multinational corporations with hundreds of items up for sale at any given time. And your chances of profits and success are just as good as theirs.

If you want to sell merchandise to consumers, eBay is a great way to do that without having to deal with the overhead expense of having a retail store. If you already have a retail operation, eBay opens up a tremendous market for you at virtually no additional cost. Millions of dollars are spent and earned on eBay every day. If you want to sell merchandise or services of any kind, you can't afford to overlook this sales channel.

According to its corporate mission statement, eBay's mission is "to provide a global trading platform where practically anyone can trade practically anything." The site has more than 147 million registered users worldwide who trade goods and services in more than 50,000 categories. In a recent survey by ACNielsen International Research, at least 724,000 Americans reported that they earned a full- or part-time living selling on eBay. In addition to those folks, another 1.5 million individuals use eBay as a means to supplement their income.

And yet, eBay has penetrated only a very small percentage of its potential market. That means the time is right for you to start selling on eBay.

Like Eating a Good Breakfast

You know how important it is to start the day right with a good breakfast, don't you? The same principle applies to selling on eBay: Get started right, and the path to profits will be much easier to navigate.

Paul Mladjenovic, a small-business specialist who also teaches classes on internet auctions, says many eBay sellers fail because they jump in without adequate research and preparation. "There are people who say, 'Why don't I just give it a shot?' and they list something. Then it doesn't work out and the listing closes without selling, and they think this is not for them," he says. In reality, many of these people could have been very successful had they taken the time to learn how to sell through online auctions before putting up their first listing.

While it is true that you learn by doing—as all the eBay sellers we spoke with agree—there are a few things you should learn before doing. After all, there's no reason for you to repeat the mistakes of others. Of course, if you already have, that's OK. Among its many benefits is the fact that eBay is a very forgiving business venue. No, there aren't any "do-overs," but there are plenty of chances to do it again—the right way.

On these pages, you're going to meet a number of successful eBay sellers, and they've all made plenty of mistakes. More important, though, is that they all do a lot of things very right—which translates into very profitable businesses.

Who Are the eBay Sellers?

Successful eBay sellers come from all backgrounds with an infinite range of experience and goals. Jonathan Garriss and David Topkins were working on Wall Street—Garriss as a portfolio manager and Topkins as a syndicate manager—when they started selling on eBay. It wasn't something they deliberately set out to do. Topkins' parents were moving out of the home he grew up in, and neither they nor he had room to store his childhood collectibles, such as baseball cards. "He didn't want to just throw them out, so he had to do something," recalls Garriss. "So we started selling them on eBay, and it was very successful. Word got around, and all of a sudden, everybody we knew who wanted to clear out their closets was coming to us to sell the stuff for them."

The pair got involved with some charities, selling items on eBay to help raise funds for worthy causes. It didn't take these two young hotshot Wall Street guys long to realize they had found an opportunity that would not only be lucrative, but also give them the sense of personal satisfaction they were missing. "Don't get me wrong—the money is great on Wall Street," Garriss says. "But there are other things you need. And this took off on its own and dragged us along with it."

Garriss and Topkins formed Gotham City Online in New York City and started selling on eBay part time in January 1999; Garriss left Wall Street to focus full time on the eBay selling operation in October of the same year, and Topkins followed in January 2000. Today, with a product line focusing on women's designer shoes and accessories, Gotham City Online's sales exceed $10 million annually and are doubling every six months.

Andrew Robinson's path to success began three years ago when he purchased two pool tables. After deciding which one he preferred, he decided to sell the other one on eBay after a friend made the suggestion. "Since I had never been on eBay before, I really questioned whether someone could actually sell a pool table," says the Columbus, Ohio, entrepreneur. But after browsing and finding people selling the same or similar products, he decided to give it a try—and was immediately hooked.

Initially, Robinson (formerly a Fortune 500 executive) and his wife ran the business from their home. But soon they were joined by partner Charles Kidder. Approximately six months later, they hired their first employee and currently have a staff of five workers who receive full benefits. "The success of eBay [enabled] us to continually grow, and we're now in our third building," Robinson says. "The current space has 15,000 square feet, plus we have an auxiliary warehouse that we use during seasonal times."

In addition to their Boston Tables eBay store, Robinson and Kidder now own nine retail furniture stores, with a total of about 65 employees.

As the IT director for CRI (Combined Resources International) in San Diego, David Lynn heads up and manages the company's online and eBay sales. He says the decision to start selling on eBay was made about a year and a half ago when CRI opened its eBay store, Combined Direct. CRI is an 11-year-old wholesale manufacturer and import distributor, primarily for large warehouse clubs such as Costco and Sam's Club, and occasionally it has overstocked items or an extra container of product that needs to be sold. "We didn't want to go through a liquidator or flood the market with prices that are below the ones for items we were still selling in the warehouse clubs, so we decided to try selling the products online," Lynn says. "And for the most part, we have had very good success with that plan." So much, in fact, that the company is now packaging products to sell exclusively online that will not be offered to its traditional warehouse customers. "We know that we have some good products, and not everyone has a local Costco to visit," says Lynn. "So we figure if we can expand the market, it will be good for all of us."

Not all successful eBay sellers fall into such high-volume operations. Sue Rudolph is a semiretired antiques dealer in Winter Park, Florida, who started selling on eBay after she closed her retail shop. "I have, as most antiques dealers do, a lot of things that have worth," says the owner of Sweet Sue's Antiques and Appraisals. "I thought it would be nice to sell some of those things and have a little extra income."

She says eBay and other online auctions have had a tremendous impact on how antiques and collectibles dealers run their businesses. When her shop was open, she considered it a good week if 100 prospective customers came through the door, and she routinely had to deal with face-to-face buyers trying to negotiate for lower prices. By contrast, she points out, on eBay, millions of potential customers are online every day, driving prices up with their bids, competing for the opportunity to buy your merchandise.

> **Fun Fact**
>
> Many successful eBay sellers got their start as a lark, posting an auction just to see what would happen, or selling a few things to make money to pay for the things they wanted to buy.

Linda Parker is a work-at-home mom in Tustin, California, who sells part time on eBay. She specializes in glassware and china, but also sells collectibles and random offbeat items. "I discovered eBay as a buyer," she says. "I began selling because I realized that if I was bidding more than I should on things, other people were, too. And I had a lot of things around the house that I wanted to get rid of but didn't think I could get much for them at a garage sale. For example, I had a Winnie the Pooh switch plate that I would have been lucky to get $2 for at a garage sale, but I sold it on eBay for $12." Her eBay activities are turning into a family business: Her 12-year-old son has been known to go through his room looking for items to sell, and her husband has even sold a few things. She predicts her 5-year-old son will follow in their footsteps.

Since she began selling on eBay in 2000, Laurie Ayers says her income has doubled every year, and she is able to be home with her children. Although she sells some new items and "gently used" things she finds at thrift stores and garage sales, her specialty is finding and reselling men's high-end designer suits and clothing. Like so many eBay sellers, the single mom in Granville, Michigan, started as a buyer. She asked a friend who was an eBay shopper to check to see if a particular item—something from a housewares line that happens to be a very popular eBay product—was up for sale. "She laughed and told me to go look for myself and hang onto my checkbook," Ayers recalls. She found what she was looking for and decided to try selling. "It was almost just for kicks—an 'I wonder if this rusty nail will sell' sort of thing. And I got hooked. I had a new baby at the time, so I sold some of her baby stuff. I sold one of her bouncy seats—it was used but in great shape—and I got more for it than a new one would cost at Target."

Liz Baker of Oviedo, Florida, began as an eBay shopper, then started selling some of her own things as well as items she found at garage sales. "Like so many people, I had plenty of things that I didn't want or need anymore, but they were in good condition, and I didn't want to just throw them out," says the work-at-home mom. "It sounds silly to say this, but I wanted my things to go to a good home. I didn't want them anymore, but I wanted someone who would appreciate them."

After a period of successfully selling books and collectibles on eBay on a part-time basis, Baker discovered Elance, which is the professional services part of eBay, and began selling her services as a virtual assistant and writer. She has also developed some of her own e-books to sell on eBay. "The opportunities on eBay are so tremendous and varied," she says. "It amazes me that I can sell my household odds and ends on the same site where I can also sell my professional services."

Gary and Susan Marler of Selma, North Carolina, consider their eBay business a hobby that allows them to earn extra cash. They began as shoppers and started selling to eliminate duplicates in their collections. "It's an easy business to do, and as you do it, you get better at it," Susan says. "For us, it has been a great way to make a little extra cash, and it has even helped us pay the bills as Gary was starting his upholstery business."

In the mountainous region of Sisters, Oregon, Peggy Webb takes a similar approach. She initially started on eBay in 2002 buying home-schooling books for her six children. "Then I thought I would have some fun selling garage-sale-type stuff from around the house," she says. "Just about the time I ran out of things to sell, I decided I was having too much fun to stop, so I started looking around for more things." Webb loves books

Tip of the Day

The FTC offers these quick tips for online auctions:

For Buyers
- ○ Identify the seller, and check the seller's feedback rating.
- ○ Do your homework. Be sure you understand what you're bidding on, its relative value, and all terms and conditions of the sale, including the seller's return policies and who pays for shipping.
- ○ Establish your top price, and stick to it.
- ○ Evaluate your payment options. If possible, use a credit card. It offers the most protection if there's a problem. Consider using an escrow service if the seller doesn't accept credit cards.

For Sellers
- ○ Provide an accurate description of the item you're selling, including all terms of the sale and who will pay shipping costs.
- ○ Respond quickly to any questions bidders may raise during the auction.
- ○ Contact the high bidder as soon as possible after the auction closes to confirm details of the sale.
- ○ Ship the merchandise as soon as you receive payment.

and settled on that niche for her eBay business, naming her store Pages-and-More. "I don't sell anything that I haven't read myself," she says.

Webb has been disabled since she was a teenager and is a member of the Disabled Online Users Association (DOUA); she attributes much of her success on eBay to that group. She says that one of the many nice things about selling on eBay is that it puts everyone on a level playing field. "Unless you read my About Me page, you wouldn't know that I walk with a cane," she says. "In a brick-and-mortar store, customers might be put off by how slowly I get around, but on the computer I can rush to my virtual bookstore when the doorbell rings."

> ## Bright Idea
>
> Make selling on eBay a family business. Get your spouse, kids, and other relatives involved in all aspects of eBay selling, from finding things to sell and handling the computer tasks necessary to post an auction to shipping the products and following up with top-notch customer service.

When Buz Moran of Long Beach, California, first started selling on eBay, he was a self-employed painter who sold collectibles on eBay as a profitable part-time hobby. "I was always a collector of stuff," he says. "eBay just happened, and I kind of fell into it like it was made for me." In his first six weeks of eBay selling, Moran made $1,800—pretty good wages for a part-time operation. "I was just buying things, not spending a lot of money but hitting home runs," he says. "I bought a bag of postcards for $5 and made more than $700 on them—one went for $142.50."

Then, a couple years ago on one of his garage sale expeditions, Moran bought a 1914 opening-day baseball pennant for the Chicago Federals for a few dollars that was in mint condition. After doing some research and talking with various collectors, he contacted Alan Rosen (aka Mr. Mint), who is well-known in the collectibles industry. Rosen purchased the pennant for a substantial amount and asked Moran to have it shipped from a local UPS store. Moran enjoyed visiting and chatting with the owners of the UPS store who showed him their operation and how things worked. He ultimately decided to open his own Mail Services Plus franchise in 2003. "I thought this was a neat business to be a part of and knew it would be a great way to tie it in with eBay because of the shipping side of it," he says. He then formed a partnership with another local eBay seller, Gary Mraz, who is a Trading Assistant (see Chapter 3 for an explanation of Trading Assistants). Together they do consignment selling for people in the area.

Georgene Harkness of Plano, Texas, started selling new and used clothing for women on eBay approximately three years ago and quickly became a top seller in her category. "I'm always in front of the computer, and one day I just decided to check eBay out," she says. "At first it was a little confusing, so I spent a lot of time getting familiar with their Help files, which really are helpful." She has never liked going to

Beware!
The world of online auctions is a rapidly evolving marketplace. As their ranks swell, shoppers are becoming increasingly sophisticated and demanding. eBay sellers who are not able to keep up with the changing market, improving their own technologies and tailoring their offerings to meet the needs of buyers, will find their businesses declining. Don't let that happen to you!

stores to shop for clothes and wanted to provide an eBay store, which she calls My New Threads, for other women who felt the same way she did.

When Bob Willey first logged onto eBay in 1998, it was primarily out of curiosity to see what all the hype was about. He quickly discovered a new and profitable outlet for the collectibles, antiques, memorabilia, and other unique items he sells through other web sites that he owns. As his online business grew, so did his knowledge about the wonderful world of eBay. Today, the Trappe, Maryland, entrepreneur is a Platinum PowerSeller and a Trading Assistant, and through his eBay business, Bob's Neat Stuff, he sells items for other people. He also teaches eBay Smart Start classes, sponsored by the Maryland Small Business Development Center, at two local colleges.

What comes through loud and clear when these sellers talk about their businesses is that eBay is about so much more than money. It's about the delight of finding a treasure and then matching it with the right buyer. It's about getting paid based on value and results, not the number of hours worked. It's about controlling your own destiny—and still more. eBay has made it possible for countless numbers of mothers to be at home with their children while earning a comfortable living—or supplementing the family's income. Sellers and buyers have connected to form business alliances as well as strong personal friendships. eBay users socialize, exchange gifts, and help each other out. After the attacks of 9/11, the Southeast Asian tsunami, and the devastating hurricanes of 2005, eBay members donated thousands of items to raise money for the families and communities hit hardest by these tragedies. Even late-night talk show host and comedian Jay Leno used eBay to auction off celebrity-autographed motorcycles that raised more than $1 million for the Red Cross. So if you're just looking for a place to do business, you've found it. And whether or not you were looking for more, you've found that, too.

What Do These Sellers Have in Common?

Your success on eBay will not be due to any one thing, but rather a combination of things. But here are a few things successful eBay sellers have in common:

- *They treat their eBay activities like a business.* You might get your start selling the occasional item on eBay the same way that you'd hold a garage sale once a year, not really caring how much you make as long as you don't lose money. But if you want a serious eBay operation that will earn you more than just pocket change, you have to treat it like a business. That means creating a separate business entity with a name, bank account, proper licenses, etc. It means finding suppliers you can count on and building solid relationships with them. It means shipping promptly, providing superior customer service, and leaving timely, accurate feedback.

- *They find a niche and build on their expertise.* It is impossible for any single person to be an expert in all the categories of merchandise on eBay. Successful eBay sellers specialize in one or two areas. "You can't possibly know the value of everything," says Mladjenovic. "The people who consistently make money, month in and month out, are the ones who specialize." They establish themselves as experts, and their knowledge is reflected in how their listings are written, the information on their About Me page, and how they respond to requests for additional information. They are generous in how they share what they know, whether it's information on their merchandise or assisting a new eBay buyer with making a purchase. Mladjenovic adds, "As soon as you start diverting from your specialty to something else, it's the same as if you started a brand-new business from scratch."

- *They are great communicators.* They know how to write auction listings that accurately and completely describe the product, shipping, payment options, return policy, and other details. They respond to questions from bidders promptly, with complete and courteous answers. They communicate with winning bidders immediately at the close of the auction and maintain that communication until the transaction is complete.

- *They are persistent and learn by doing.* Successful eBay sellers don't give up easily. When an auction doesn't go as expected, they figure out what to do differently the next time for better results. They learn from their mistakes. And even when things are going well, they are always trying to figure out how to make them better.

From Recreation to Business

Selling on eBay is one of the easiest ways to turn your hobby or special interests into a business. Think about it: Whatever you enjoy doing, you have a degree of expertise and experience in—and you can translate that to dollars on eBay.

Most of the eBay sellers we interviewed had been buying and selling on eBay just for fun before getting serious about their businesses, and they all knew of others who had done the same thing. However, just because you enjoy your particular hobby and eBay shopping, don't make the mistake of thinking this will be just a lot of fun and games. One of the biggest pitfalls of taking this route to business ownership is failing to make the complete transition from amateur to professional.

No matter how enjoyable you find the process of buying and selling at auctions, you are selling a product your customers are paying money for, and you must respect the fact that this is a business transaction. You need to take yourself seriously and run your company like the professional operation you want it to be.

One of the most important issues you'll have to deal with is record-keeping. Whether you're new to online selling or you've been doing it for a while, consider these suggestions:

- *Open a separate checking account for the business.* Your bank account balance is a quick and easy way to see how well you're doing, but you won't have a clear picture unless you're using an account that is strictly for business income and expenses. Linda Parker, the part-time Tustin, California, eBay seller, says the smartest thing she ever did in her business was opening that separate bank account. "For a long time, I just threw everything into our joint checking account, but it became very confusing with all these deposits and withdrawals, and I couldn't stand it anymore," she recalls. "Having everything separate makes it easy for me to tell whether I'm making as much money as I feel like I am. For instance, I may have a bunch of auctions end at the same time, and all the payments come in close together, and it seems like a lot of revenue. But with a separate account, it's easy to see what my costs were and how much real profit I made."

- *Get a credit card for the business.* You may not be able to get the card in the business name, and you may not be able to charge all your business purchases (for example, garage sale shopping requires cash), but at least have one card that is used exclusively for business expenses. This helps you keep your records in order and—if the card is in the business name—helps you establish business credit.

- *Invest in a retirement plan.* Beyond the long-term benefits, a retirement plan offers some short-term advantages. You'll not only reduce your current taxes, but if you are a homebased sole proprietor, the fact that you show a retirement plan on your income tax return indicates to the IRS that you are serious about your business, not just trying to take some questionable deductions.

- *Document your equipment.* Of course, anything you buy for your business after you start it is a deductible expense. However, if you purchased the equipment you use to sell on eBay (computer, printer, digital camera, scales, etc.) prior to starting your business and can prove the cost involved, you may be able to deduct those expenses on your tax return after you've formed your company. Talk to your tax advisor for specifics on how to do this.

- *Figure out how much it actually costs you to sell an item.* Besides the cost of the merchandise, calculate your overhead (the cost of maintaining a place to work); the time it takes you to write up your auction description, take photographs, and get the listing posted; packaging; freight; special handling; and any other expenses. Be especially careful about tracking your time; too many business owners in all industries fail to give their time the value it deserves.

Use the "Start-Up Checklist" on page 12 to make sure you tackle the goal of selling on eBay in an organized, well-thought-out way.

More than Stuff and Services

In addition to being a great tool to use to start your own business, eBay is also a place where you might find an existing business to buy. Thousands of businesses are up for sale on eBay each month. Of course, many are iffy at best ("make money at home with your computer")—some listings in this category are instruction manuals and/or equipment rather than actual established businesses—but there are some real businesses for sale on eBay.

For a legitimate business or franchise, don't expect the process to be as quick as an auction for consumer merchandise. Buying or selling a business requires a lot of research, documentation, and negotiation. But eBay can still be a great way for people who are interested in buying or selling a business to hook up.

Buy First—Sell Later

Before you start selling on eBay, make a few purchases. "Before you try to sell anything on eBay, first take a look as a shopper for [what you want to sell] and see what other listings are like," says Mladjenovic. You'll learn firsthand how the system works and be able to put yourself in your customers' shoes. You don't have to spend a lot of money, and chances are you'll find things that you'd buy elsewhere anyway.

Another benefit of starting out as a shopper is that it gives you a chance to build a history under your user ID and earn some positive feedback (the value of which is explained in later chapters) so buyers will feel more comfortable with you later on when you start selling.

"Buy from a variety of different, experienced sellers and see how they handle their auctions from beginning to end," advises Susan Marler. "Imitate—but don't duplicate—the good sellers, and learn what not to do from the bad experiences."

Start-Up Checklist

As exciting as eBay is, don't let it lure you into the deep end of the pool until you know how to swim. Use this checklist to get started.

❑ Register on eBay.

❑ Decide what type of eBay business you want to start.

❑ Research your market.

❑ Set goals for your business.

❑ Develop a plan to achieve your goals.

❑ Do some shopping on eBay.

❑ Learn how to use eBay and its tools.

❑ Become familiar with eBay's policies.

❑ Create an About Me page.

❑ Open a business bank account.

❑ Register on PayPal and add merchant tools to accept credit cards and e-checks.

❑ Set up your payment system to accept other forms of payment (e.g., checks and money orders).

❑ Choose a location, whether it's a room at home or a commercial building.

❑ Set up a record-keeping system.

❑ Obtain necessary licenses.

❑ Find sources for merchandise to sell.

❑ Set up your shipping system.

❑ Learn how to write a good description for your auction.

❑ Get the necessary equipment (either scanner or digital camera) to take good pictures.

❑ Auction a few items to gain experience.

❑ Collect payment.

❑ Ship the merchandise promptly.

❑ Post feedback.

❑ Auction more items!

A Day in the Life
What It's Like to Be an eBay Seller

So what's it like to have a business that sells on eBay? The sellers we spoke with agreed: It's a lot of work— and a lot of fun.

A Day in the Life

Because there is no such thing as a typical eBay seller or a typical eBay business, there is no such thing as a typical day for an eBay seller. How they spend their days depends on the type of operation they have.

Gotham City Online's Jonathan Garriss says both he and his partner typically work 12-hour days, six days a week. And though that sounds like a lot, he points out, "When we first started, we were working 15 or 16 hours a day, seven days a week."

With a staff of 30, Garriss doesn't spend his time listing auctions, taking pictures, or packing items to be shipped. Instead, he figures about 30 percent of a typical day is spent on operational issues, including monitoring financials, reviewing payments, and troubleshooting. The remainder of his time is focused on business development, building relationships with suppliers and customers, and developing systems to create a more efficient operation.

A snapshot of a smaller-scale operation looks both similar and different. Part-time eBay seller Linda Parker spends an average of two hours a day monitoring listings, answering questions from bidders, packing sold items, going to the post office, and doing other administrative chores. One or two days a week, she spends an additional three or four hours shopping at garage sales, estate sales, and thrift shops for things to sell. Her profits are modest—just a few hundred dollars a month—but she enjoys the work, the extra income, and the fact that she's able to be at home with her children every day.

Laurie Ayers averages three hours a day on eBay tasks. The Marlers spend about an hour or two a day online managing their auctions, corresponding with customers, and sending invoices. They spend about two to three hours each week on packing and shipping, and another two to three hours looking for merchandise to sell.

It's no surprise that the higher the volume of sales of the eBay sellers we talked to, the more systematic their approach is. Those who started out selling on eBay as a lark became more systematic as they got more serious about their businesses. Starting with a system will mean faster profits.

All about eBay

Mention eBay to 10 people, and at least one of them is likely to say something like, "I went on the site once, and I was just overwhelmed. There was too much on it." The fact is eBay can be overwhelming at first, especially if you don't have any goals in mind when you first log on. But it doesn't take long to get comfortable with the site and all it has to offer.

Perhaps the most important thing to keep in mind about eBay is that it is constantly changing and evolving. In just the time it took to research and write this guide, we saw many changes and enhancements on eBay. And most of those changes involve making eBay more user-friendly and less intimidating.

Beware!
"The main strength of eBay is that there are millions of buyers and millions of sellers [on the site] 24 hours a day," says consultant Paul Mladjenovic. "But the main weakness of eBay is that there are millions of buyers and millions of sellers every day."

It's important to understand that eBay is not just one giant web site—though it's definitely giant, it's actually a collection of sites offering sellers and buyers a variety of options. In addition to basic online auctions, those sites include:

- eBay Motors: where vehicles of all kinds are bought and sold
- eBay Stores: where sellers can set up a fixed site on which to sell their goods
- PayPal: eBay's payment processing service
- Giving Works: a program for listing charity auctions where some or all of the proceeds are donated to nonprofit organizations

Birds of a Feather

Many eBay sellers network with one another through various forums, groups, and e-mail lists. In addition to the different communities found on eBay, you can find online networking opportunities throughout the internet. For example, single mom and eBay seller Laurie Ayers is a member of two Yahoo! groups, "Staying at Home" and "Christian eBay Moms." She credits the support from those online communities as the primary reason for her eBay success and growth. "You've got to have support and encouragement," she says. "If you are left on your own, you are going to miss out on some valuable information." She says her online colleagues help motivate her when she's feeling down. "I've met some wonderful people online who I consider my friends, not just other sellers. There are more benefits to eBay than just moving your goods."

Sources for online groups include Google Groups (go to www.google.com and click on the "Groups" tab), Yahoo! Groups (go to http://groups.yahoo.com), and Topica (go to www.lists.topica.com).

- Live Auctions: where buyers can bid on merchandise at a live auction as it's happening
- Elance: eBay's marketplace for professional services
- Half.com: another eBay portal to buy or sell items at reduced, fixed prices
- eBay Business: a marketplace especially for business buyers and sellers
- ProStores: an independent site that comes fully loaded with e-commerce and merchant capabilities and easily integrates with the eBay marketplace
- Epinions.com: helps consumers make informed buying decisions by offering a platform for other people to post their opinions and reviews on specific products
- Rent.com: helps match landlords and tenants, as well as roommates; searches can also be performed for moving supplies and services
- Shopping.com: allows buyers to do comparison shopping with a multitude of online merchants to find the best deals
- Skype: eBay's most recent acquisition allows people to make long-distance phone calls over the internet at a reduced cost

eBay Policies

Complete details on current eBay policies can be found on eBay's web site, so we won't go into all of them here. However, there are some you should know about before you begin buying and selling on eBay.

- *No kids allowed.* eBay requires that all users be at least 18 years of age. If your children want to sell things on eBay, you have to do it for them—and be responsible for the transaction.
- *Nonpaying bidder.* Bidders who win auctions but fail to follow through with the transaction face consequences. Nonpaying bidders will receive two warnings from eBay before they are suspended. Continued violations after reinstatement will result in an indefinite suspension. Of course, eBay understands that there may be legitimate reasons when a bidder doesn't complete a transaction, such as serious illness, emergencies, acts of nature, and computer problems. Nonpaying bidders can appeal the warnings they receive from eBay if they believe their circumstances warrant special consideration. When a bidder doesn't pay, the seller may request a credit from eBay for their final value fee.
- *Nonperforming seller.* Significantly misrepresenting an item by not meeting the terms and item description in the auction or failing to deliver an item for which you accepted payment is a violation of eBay policies and may also be considered criminal fraud.
- *Duplicate auctions.* A seller can have up to ten listings for identical items at any one time, but no more. eBay recommends selling identical items through

Dutch auctions or eBay stores (covered later), rather than through individual auctions.

- *Outages.* When the eBay system experiences service outages, there is a structure in place to compensate users with credits on listing fees and/or listing extensions, based on the type and length of outage.

- *Soliciting off-site sales.* You may not circumvent eBay fees by using contact information obtained from eBay or any eBay service to complete a sale outside eBay.
- *Threats.* eBay policies prohibit making threats of physical harm to another user.
- *Profanity:* The use of language that is racist, hateful, sexual, or obscene in nature in a public area is prohibited on eBay.
- *Prohibited and restricted items.* As an eBay user, you are ultimately responsible for making sure that the items you buy and sell on eBay are both legal according to all applicable jurisdictions and permitted by eBay policies.
- *Keyword spamming.* Sellers are not allowed to put unrelated brand names or other inappropriate keywords in an auction title or description in an attempt to draw attention to that listing.

If you violate an eBay policy by either your action or the content of your auctions, you will typically receive an informational alert explaining the violation and detailing any further action to be taken on your part. When deemed appropriate, eBay will end the auction and your listing fee will be refunded.

For serious or repeated violations of eBay rules, a user may be indefinitely suspended. Though indefinitely suspended users may be reinstated by eBay at its discretion, eBay also has the right to determine at any time that the suspension is permanent.

Suspended users may not register with eBay or use eBay's site in any way during the period of the suspension. When a user has failed to abide by this restriction, eBay will refer the situation for criminal prosecution.

It's a Very Safe Neighborhood

When you're considering opening a brick-and-mortar store, one of the things you think about when choosing your location is how safe the neighborhood might be. That's an issue you need to keep in mind when operating online, too. Though not totally without risk, as a venue for business operations, eBay is extraordinarily safe.

Most eBay users—like most people—are honest. But you don't have to just hope that you aren't dealing with the rare bad apple. eBay's feedback system gives you the opportunity to check the reputation of both buyers and sellers before you agree to a particular transaction.

In addition, all eBay transactions are covered by the eBay Standard Purchase Protection Program, which reimburses buyers up to $200 (less $25 to cover processing) for items they don't receive or that they are dissatisfied with, if they are unable to work the problem out with the seller. If the item was paid for through PayPal, buyers may be eligible for compensation up to $1,000 through PayPal's Buyer Protection Program. eBay's SafeHarbor and Square Trade also have systems in place to help protect users when disputes arise or misuse of the system occurs.

Does eBay have its detractors? Certainly. Read some of the articles criticizing eBay, and you'll wonder how the company can stay afloat until tomorrow. But no company is perfect. When you look at the big picture, you'll see an organization that is financially sound with a clear plan for the future.

Is the eBay site absolutely perfect and flawless? No. As do all internet sites, eBay suffers from occasional glitches and outages—that's why they have an outage policy. However, it's up to you to monitor your auctions and report any problems. Also, if a service failure on eBay's part has a negative impact on your auctions, request the appropriate credit on your listing fees.

Now that we've completed this overview of eBay as an organization and an opportunity, let's get down to the nitty-gritty of doing business on the site. We'll begin with taking a look at what you can sell.

What Can You
Sell Online?

So what kind of merchandise should you sell? A lot of eBay sellers start out selling odds and ends they have around the house—and for good reason. For items that are in good condition, you'll probably get more money for them on eBay than at a garage sale. You probably have plenty of stuff that you'll never miss and you really don't need to store or dust anymore. And it's a relatively risk-free way to test the waters of eBay selling.

If you can't bear to part with anything you already have, start with products you know and have experience with. Choose things that have demonstrable market demand (that is, you know people are buying them). Don't make the mistake of selling only things you like, or the trendiest, coolest things you can find. If your goal is to make a profit—and it should be!—then you need to be selling things people will buy.

Currently, the category with the greatest level of growth is eBay Motors. However, we are not discussing the topic of selling cars online as an eBay opportunity because it's one thing to put your own car up for sale; it's altogether something else to start a business as a car dealer, and that's beyond the scope of this book. The next biggest-selling category is consumer electronics, followed closely by computers (both desktops and laptops); clothing and accessories; books, movies, and music; collectibles; home and garden; sports; toys; jewelry and watches; cameras and photo; and business and industrial. Each of these categories generates an estimated $1 billion or more a year in business.

Just about anything you sell on eBay has the potential to be profitable—or not, depending on how you run your business. And eBay sellers have been amazingly creative at coming up with items to auction. One woman gathered all the junk she found in the cushions of her sofa—gum wrappers, broken pencils, pen caps, peanut shells, etc.—and photographed it neatly arranged on a piece of velvet cloth, then put it up for auction and sold it for about $15. Another top seller was a "mother-in-law Barbie doll" that came with luggage, printed voodoo chants, and stickpins.

If you are considering selling an item, do a search on eBay and see if that product or similar ones are being offered for sale. If the market is saturated, you may want to reconsider trying to sell that product. At the same time, if absolutely no one else is offering the product for sale, you need to figure out if that's because no one else has thought of it or if it's because no one will buy the item.

Depending on the category, seeing a lot of similar items up for sale may work in your favor or against you. For example, you may see a lot of the same item pop up in response to a search because people are buying. Or, observes antiques seller Sue Rudolph, "It might also mean the market is flooded and nobody wants it." You have to do more than just count the listings, she says. Look at the individual auctions and see if people are bidding on the items—that will give you an indication of the strength of the market. Then check the completed auctions for the item you searched for. That will tell you what the item is selling for (if, in fact, it's selling at all).

Collectible items that are not easy to find will naturally have less competition than commonplace merchandise and will probably bring in more money. However, if you're going to have a steady source of income, you also need a steady source of supply for whatever you're selling. Hard-to-find items may be more profitable on a per-sale basis, but focusing on those items may limit the number of sales—and therefore the amount of money—you can make on eBay.

If you really enjoy trading in those hard-to-find treasures, consider a mix of related items. Also, develop methods to reduce the amount of time you search for those items. For example, Laurie Ayers previously sold a lot of children's items—mostly things that were very common but in relatively high demand. However, she has found her niche with used designer men's Italian suits. While they aren't quite in the same category as a rare antique, they're still not extremely common. She finds them at thrift stores and occasionally at garage sales. "Once I found three Giorgio Armani suits for a total of $30, and I sold them for almost $600 total," she says. Because she knows exactly what she's looking for, her thrift store excursions are fast and efficient. Men's ties also sell well. "I paid a quarter for a tie once, and sold it for almost $40." She concedes that you often have to sort through a lot of junk to find such treasures, but if you've done your research and you know what you're looking for, you can usually do it quickly. "There are a lot of good suits out there," she says, "but I limit my search to just the exclusive brands. If the label is not on my list, then I don't bother to pick it up."

> **Smart Tip** — *Tip...*
>
> Brand names sell. New or used, people prefer to buy brands they recognize and trust. That means selling brand names is likely to be easier and more profitable than off-brands. But before promoting someone else's trademark, be sure to familiarize yourself with eBay's Verified Rights Owner (VeRO) Program so that your listings are legal.

Deciding What to Sell

Whether you have a specific product line in mind or are still trying to come up with some ideas for what you can sell on eBay, consider these issues:

- *Cost.* How much will the item cost you? There's more to cost than simply the price on the item—do you have the cash required to make the purchase or are you going to have to borrow money (and therefore pay interest) to acquire the inventory? Will there be any additional expenses, such as shipping to you or repairs if the item is not in saleable condition?

- *Storage.* Do you have room to adequately and safely store the item while you are waiting for it to sell?

- *Shipping.* What are the labor and cost issues associated with shipping the item to your customer once it sells? Is it very fragile, an unusual shape, or extremely heavy? These are issues that can make shipping a challenge.
- *Product life cycle.* How long can you expect the demand for the item to continue? You may have something that is wildly successful today, but next year you won't be able to pay people to take it away from you. Beanie Babies and other fad collectibles are a great example of this. Some high-tech items are also at risk of having a short life cycle due to technology advances. If you pay attention to product life cycles, you can maximize your profits while the item is hot and avoid getting stuck with excess inventory when the demand declines.
- *Season.* When you put an item up for sale on eBay, consider the time of year. Heavy coats and sweaters don't sell well in the spring and summer. Lawn and garden equipment is not going to move as well in the winter as it will in the summer. If you have room to store items, you can make a nice profit buying off-season items and holding them until they'll sell.

> **Smart Tip** **Tip...**
> Consultant Paul Mladjenovic advises buying from people who do not understand the value of the items as well as you do (and are therefore willing to sell for less), but selling to people who do understand value and are willing to pay what the item is worth.

Where Will You Find What You'll Sell?

One of the most exciting things about selling on eBay is that merchandise that will sell for a profit is virtually everywhere!

- *Your home.* Start by looking around your own home at the stuff that's collecting dust on shelves or stashed in the back of closets, or in the attic or garage.
- *Flea markets.* Flea markets can be a tremendous source of bargain-priced merchandise that will sell on eBay.
- *Garage and yard sales.* Savvy eBay sellers can make a comfortable living spending one or two days a week shopping garage sales for items that will fetch many times what they cost when auctioned on eBay.
- *Estate sales.* If a professional is already handling the estate sale, you're not as likely to get really great bargains. But if

> **Bright Idea**
> If you've received a gift you don't want and can't return, sell it on eBay.

Brother, Will You Take a Deposit?

If you find a great deal on something you know you can sell on eBay but you don't have the cash to buy it outright, offer a small deposit to hold the goods for 10 to 14 days. Then post your auction for seven days, and when it closes and the item has sold, pick it up and pay the balance due then.

Do this only when you're buying from a seller you know and trust, and when you have carefully inspected the merchandise and are completely confident about authenticity and quality. If for any reason the item doesn't sell, you'll likely lose your deposit—but that's better than getting stuck with a high-priced item in your inventory that won't move.

you have access to a truck and storage, you can advertise that you buy entire estates. When you make such a purchase, select what will sell best on eBay, put those items up for auction, and then sell the rest through other channels.

- *Established retailers.* Stores need a way to move items that aren't selling. Once Gotham City Online was established, Jonathan Garriss was able to approach retailers and offer to help them solve their overstock problems by selling those items on a consignment basis on eBay. Eventually, he began purchasing that inventory outright.

- *Discount stores.* Look for clearance items at discount department and drug stores. Susan Marler routinely buys women's accessories at the end of the season and stores them until the following year. "I buy out of season, and I have found great bargains on clearance sales," she says.

- *Bankruptcy and going-out-of-business sales.* Companies that need to get rid of inventory quickly because they are moving or closing can be great sources for products.

- *Online auctions.* eBay and other auction venues can often be a good place to find items. Look for auction titles with misspelled words that most browsers will overlook, or listings that have poor photographs or descriptions that buyers will be reluctant to bid on. You can also purchase inventory lots that can later be split up and sold individually for a profit.

- *Friends and family.* Tell people you know not to throw anything away. Laurie Ayers says that members of her church will give her things they are going to throw away or donate to charity, and if she can sell them on eBay, she does.

Buying from Wholesalers

As your business grows, you may choose to start buying from wholesale sources and selling on eBay at retail. This can be very profitable, but only if you choose the wholesaler wisely.

The internet is full of opportunities to buy lists of wholesalers, often for just a few dollars. Save your money. You can get the same quality of information (or maybe even slightly better) for free by using any of the popular search engines and plugging in keywords such as "wholesale," "manufacturer," or "drop ship." But even that is not the best route to take.

Beware!
Avoid wholesalers and distributors who charge an account setup fee or any other fee, or who want to restrict the products you sell. Legitimate companies make money from selling their products, not from charging administrative fees.

Instead, be more specific in your approach. Think about the type of products you want to sell, and then look for manufacturers, wholesalers, and distributors you can work with. Find companies whose products meet your quality expectations, that have prices and terms you can work with, and that deliver the service level you want to provide your customers. Get sample products so you can see the quality yourself. Some companies send free samples, while others charge a nominal fee—either way, don't try to sell something you've never seen. Be sure it is truly worth what you expect it to sell for.

Trappe, Maryland, eBay seller Bob Willey encourages sellers who plan to use wholesalers to do their due diligence and thoroughly research the company as well as the products they want to sell. "If you discover an item that is hard to find, then you have a good source for making money," he says. "But if everyone else is selling the same thing, your chances of making money are greatly reduced."

You may wonder why wholesalers aren't just selling their merchandise on eBay themselves for a greater profit. Some of them may be, but most legitimate wholesalers prefer to avoid the retail market and focus on the type of selling they do best, which is to sell their products to a retailer who will then sell to the public. Consultant Paul Mladjenovic explains that this is how they reach a wider market with fewer resources than if they tried to set up their own retail structure.

As you consider what to sell on eBay, keep this in mind: If you wouldn't buy shoddy, off-brand, imported merchandise for yourself, why would someone else want to buy it from you?

Willey advises sellers to familiarize themselves with eBay's drop-shipping policy, especially if the wholesaler is shipping for you. "If you sell things that you don't have in your possession, just remember that according to eBay, *you* as the seller are responsible for having the product available and delivered," he cautions.

Be sure you're dealing with a true manufacturer, wholesaler, or distributor, and not another middleman who is marking up their prices and increasing your costs. Ask for and check references. You want to talk with others who are buying from these sources. In addition, check with the Better Business Bureau, any industry associations, the consumer protection agency of the state in which the supplier is located, and any other source that may be able to verify their claims.

Legitimate manufacturers, wholesalers, and distributors will also want information about you, including proof that you are a legitimate business and that you have any necessary licenses and tax identification numbers. (You'll learn more about these issues in Chapter 8.) A supplier who doesn't ask for this information is probably a middleman whose ethics couldn't stand up to moderate, much less close, scrutiny. Also, the discussion on purchasing in Chapter 11 applies not only to equipment for your business but to your inventory as well.

Keep this in mind: You're able to set up shop on the internet for a very small investment, and your goal is to build a legitimate business. Don't you think scam artists know how easy it is to create an internet presence? Of course they do. Don't become one of their victims.

Can You Compete Against the Superstores?

In many ways, the internet is a great equalizer. When you're selling on eBay, you're keeping company with retail giants such as Sears, Sharper Image, Disney, Palm, Wickes Lumber, Motorola, the Golf Channel Pro Shop, and more. And there's absolutely no reason you can't capture a reasonable share of the market these companies target.

Of course, you're also going to be competing against brick-and-mortar retail outlets, many with hundreds, if not thousands, of locations and the ability to buy in vast quantities at great prices. Don't let that scare you. At the same time, don't try to beat Wal-Mart at its own game. Don't try to sell the same products when there's no possible way you can match Wal-Mart's price and still make a profit. Instead, find a niche and a need that isn't being met by Wal-Mart (or other discount stores). Once you get a customer, offer service so great that they'll want to deal with you again and again.

Keep this in mind: Superstores carry a lot of products, but they can't possibly carry everything, and they usually only stock a few variations of each item. There are literally hundreds of thousands of items that are not being sold in a superstore that people want to buy.

Another point to remember: Don't make price your primary selling point. Certainly many people are looking for bargains when

> **Smart Tip** *Tip...*
> When buying, know what your top price is before you begin negotiating, and don't go over it. When selling, know your minimum. Always keep these figures in mind during your negotiations.

they shop on eBay, but not all eBay buyers are low-price shoppers. You should stress the benefits of your merchandise over and above price. There will always be someone who can sell for less than you.

Sharpen Your Negotiating Skills

When you're buying, you want to pay the lowest price possible—and when you're selling, of course, you want the highest price possible. That's why it's important that you know the market value of the products you intend to sell before you buy them. There's no real negotiation involved in selling through an eBay auction because you decide the minimum you'll accept, and the person who bids the highest amount above that wins. But when you're buying, your negotiation skills can mean the difference between a profit and a loss. In fact, more than one eBay seller told us their profits are actually made when they purchase their inventory—they just don't receive those dollars until the sale is complete.

Regardless of whom you're buying from—an individual, a small company, or a huge corporation—find out if there's any room for negotiation on the deal. The easiest way to do that is to simply ask. And if the merchandise price is firm, find out if you can deal on payment terms, shipping costs, delivery arrangements, or any other aspect of the transaction.

Scavenger Hunt

As the economy cycles, it's easy to pick up bargains from distressed individuals and companies, and the internet has made finding, buying ,and selling these items much easier than in the past. You might think that easier accessibility and availability would drive prices down, but that's not necessarily the case. For example, let's say you live in a small Midwestern town and you find a piece of modestly priced art at an estate sale. You've done your homework and you recognize the value of the piece, but you also know that no one locally would be interested in buying it. However, with eBay and other online auctions, a collector in Los Angeles or New York who is willing to pay fair value can easily see the piece and buy it from you at a handsome profit. Remember that online auctions and other internet sales avenues have opened up a wide range of markets that have a tremendous profit potential.

Always offer less than the asking price. You can always come up on your price if the seller refuses to budge and you still want the deal, but you can't go down once you've made an offer. Of course, don't just offer less—explain why you're offering less, and do it in a way that won't offend the seller. For example, don't say, "You want $200 for this? There's no way this junk is worth more than $150." Instead, say something like "I understand why you feel that this merchandise is worth $200, but considering the market and what it's going to take for me to resell it, I can only offer you $150." Then be quiet and wait for a response.

Another effective technique is to let the seller name a lower price. Let's say the item you want is marked at $50. Just ask, "What's the lowest amount you'd take for this?" The seller may say, "$50," in which case you can counter with a lower figure, pay the asking amount, or walk away. Or the seller may say, "Well, I really want $50, but I'd let it go for $35." If you'd been hoping to get it for $40, you just made $5 on the deal.

In any situation, whether you're buying a salt shaker at a garage sale or a truckload of electronics from a major manufacturer, treat everyone involved with respect, listen to the other person's point of view and be sure you understand it correctly, and work toward a win-win solution.

Consignment Selling

Consignment selling is a great way to make money on eBay without having to invest in inventory. You simply sell other people's stuff—typically antiques and collectibles, but it could be anything—and when the transaction is complete, you pay those people the amount for which the item sold, less a fee for your trouble. Consignment fees can range from as low as 10 percent to as high as 30 percent or more. When Garriss first started selling items his friends were cleaning out of their closets, he did it on a consignment basis with a 50-50 split of revenue after expenses.

Where can you find items to sell on consignment? Look around and be creative. Collectors who don't want to bother learning how to do online auctions may be happy to consign items to you for sale on eBay. Small specialty retail store owners or crafters might consider a consignment arrangement. Even thrift stores and retail consignment shops could let you sell

Beware!
When buying luxury items such as designer accessories and high-end jewelry to sell on eBay, ask to see the seller's driver's license and make a copy of it for your files. Also, have the seller sign a bill of sale that clearly describes the goods involved. This will protect you from criminal prosecution if it turns out that the merchandise has been stolen.

some of their merchandise on eBay for them. You can also spread the word by telling everyone you know that you're willing to sell things on consignment on eBay for them.

A good policy to use when selling on consignment is to insist on taking possession of the articles. Here's why: Let's say you find an antique desk the owner wants to sell. You sign a consignment contract, take pictures of the desk, and go home and list it on eBay, leaving the desk with the owner. When the auction is complete, the buyer sends you the money, and you call the owner to arrange to ship the desk. But he tells you he has changed his mind about selling.

Now, you have a contract, which means you can take the issue to court and probably win. But is your buyer going to wait four to six months for you to get an injunction forcing the owner to turn over the desk? Probably not.

If you had possession of the desk before you put the auction up, this couldn't happen. Even if the owner changes his mind, you are in control when you have the merchandise in your own hands. Let's say that in the above scenario the owner called while the auction was in progress to say he wanted the desk back. You could explain that you have a contract and he is bound by it. Or, since the auction hasn't closed yet, you could offer to cancel the contract if the owner is willing to compensate you for your costs and time. However, once the auction has closed, you are contractually obligated to sell the item. So protect yourself by taking possession of consignment items.

"We take possession of all the merchandise we have for sale," says Garriss. "That's what allows us to do things like give special discounts on shipping to people who buy more than one item. It also allows us to control delivery and customer service."

It's best to have a written agreement for all your consignment sales, even when you're dealing with a friend—or perhaps, especially when you're dealing with a friend. Writing it all down prevents any possible misunderstandings. Your agreement should include the commission amount (usually a percentage of the sale price), who pays selling expenses and what those are likely to include, a minimum sale price if applicable, when and how payment will be made, and anything else that may be relevant.

If you've agreed to sell a jumbled pile of items, consider charging an hourly fee for sorting and cleaning. If the owner balks, explain that you are a professional, this is your business, and if he doesn't want to compensate you fairly for your time, he can find someone else or do the job himself.

Trading Assistant

Take consignment selling to a new level by becoming a Trading Assistant. eBay created this program for people who want help selling their items online. By the time you finish reading this book, you should be quite comfortable selling your own merchandise on eBay. And when you've gained some experience, you can make some extra money selling items for others who can't—or don't want to—do it themselves.

eBay defines Trading Assistants as "experienced eBay sellers who have indicated their willingness to sell items for others for a fee. All terms will be negotiated between Trading Assistants and their clients."

To become a Trading Assistant, you must have sold four or more items within the past 30 days and have a feedback rating of at least 50 with a minimum of 97 percent positive feedback. This status must be maintained to keep a visible presence in the Trading Assistants Directory, which is a great marketing tool for consignment selling. Set up a Trading Assistant profile page on eBay describing your experience, what you're willing to sell, and the services you provide. Trading Assistants typically negotiate their fees with their clients on an individual basis.

Beware!
The Consumer Product Safety Commission bans the sale of goods that may be dangerous to consumers. Visit www.cpsc.gov for more information.

Bob Willey has operated as a Trading Assistant with great success for two and a half years. "People will find you using the eBay Trading Assistants Directory," he says. "Once your name is established, it can keep you very busy." He enjoys managing a range of products from many different sources. "I really get a kick out of watching a listing doing great," Willey confesses, "like the boat I sold for a gentleman a few months ago—a 1996 Formula 330SS 33-foot cigarette boat with dual diesels that went for $63,100!" For extra help learning to be a profitable Trading Assistant and consignment seller, Willey recommends using the information and equipment at www.foundvalue.com. The site offers one-on-one mentoring, online resources, and tools to set up your eBay business.

As a Trading Assistant, you are responsible for representing the product accurately in the listing and being sure it meets eBay's listing policies. Because you are listing the product, eBay considers you the seller, with all the accompanying responsibilities and obligations.

To sign up to become a Trading Assistant, go to the eBay Services page and click on "Trading Assistant."

Trading Posts

Most Trading Assistants operate from their homes or warehouses; however, eBay has made it possible for Trading Assistants to operate out of retail storefronts. Trading Posts serve as drop-off points for consignors who bring in their items during traditional business hours without an appointment. If the Trading Assistants have a special agreement with eBay, they can also offer copying, mailing, and/or shipping services. To qualify for this designation and promote the eBay brand, users must be Trading Assistants with 98 percent positive feedback scores of 500 or more. They must also have eBay sales of at least $25,000 per month.

It goes without saying that running a brick-and-mortar store involves greater overhead costs than working from your home, but if you are selling a large volume of goods on consignment and want to expand that part of your business, the investment may be worth it because a storefront makes you more visible. If you don't want to start from scratch, consider purchasing a franchise that operates as an eBay Trading Post, such as QuikDrop, Auction Drop, or iSOLD It on eBay.

Trading Posts don't have to be retail storefronts, though. As a Platinum PowerSeller with an excellent record as a Trading Assistant, Willey's business qualifies as a Trading Post that he operates from his home. "I have about 700 square feet that is isolated from the rest of the house," he says. "It has a separate entrance and private office that I use for my eBay business."

Special Rules for Selling Jewelry

The FTC requires that you make accurate and truthful claims about jewelry you offer for sale and has issued guides to help you. The guides explain how to describe gold, silver, platinum, pewter, diamonds, gemstones, and pearls, and also outline what information you must disclose so that consumers are not misled. For example, if you are selling synthetic or imitation gemstones, you must clearly tell the consumer that the stone is not natural. If you are selling pearls, you must indicate if they are cultured or imitation. Copies of the FTC's Jewelry Guides can be obtained on the agency's web site, www.ftc.gov.

Know and Heed the Restrictions

Considering the mind-boggling number and variety of items available on eBay, you might think that absolutely anything can be sold on this auction site. Not true.

eBay's policies very specifically bar the sale of any illegal item, and the company also has a detailed list of restrictions. (See "Is That Legal?" starting on page 31 for a list of prohibited, questionable, and potentially infringing items.) Violate these restrictions, and at the very least your auction will be ended. At most, you'll find yourself suspended from eBay and possibly facing legal action. When the auction involves illegal activity, eBay will report the seller to the proper authorities.

For example, it didn't take long for items billed as debris from the space shuttle Columbia to appear on eBay—nor did it take long for those listings to be pulled from the site. Of course, taking part of an aircraft involved in an accident is a federal offense, which would also make attempting to sell pieces of Columbia subject to federal prosecution. But beyond the legal aspects, eBay often pulls listings that attempt to capitalize on a tragedy, such as when people attempted to sell pieces of the World

Trade Center and Pentagon after 9/11 and when some set up fictitious charity auctions in the wake of Hurricane Katrina.

eBay's customer service team regularly checks the site for merchandise that might be restricted or prohibited. They also respond quickly to user complaints about an item that may violate policies, so if you suspect a listing violates eBay's policies, report it.

In the case of illegal items such as stolen goods, eBay cooperates with authorities. There have been instances where authorities have asked the auction site to leave a particular listing up in what amounts to a cyber-sting. Police officers bid on the item, making sure they win the auction. When they make arrangements to receive the merchandise, the arrest is made.

When it comes to dealing with policy violations, eBay tends to give users the benefit of the doubt. Typically, you'll get a notice explaining what you've done wrong and essentially telling you not to do it again. Repeated violations will likely result in a short-term suspension of your eBay account. Serious violations and chronic offenders may be indefinitely suspended.

Is That Legal?

The following list details items that are prohibited, questionable, and potentially infringing. If you're not sure your item is acceptable on eBay, check out the policies in the Help section of the site.

Prohibited

The following items may not, under any circumstances, be listed on eBay:

- ○ Airline and transit-related items
- ○ Alcohol
- ○ Animals and wildlife products
- ○ Catalog and URL sales
- ○ Counterfeit currency and stamps
- ○ Counterfeit items
- ○ Credit cards
- ○ Drugs and drug paraphernalia
- ○ Embargoed goods and items made in prohibited countries
- ○ Firearms
- ○ Fireworks
- ○ Gift cards

▲

Is That Legal? (continued)

- ○ Government IDs and licenses
- ○ Human parts and remains
- ○ Links to other web sites (except as allowed in eBay's policies)
- ○ Lock-picking devices
- ○ Lottery tickets
- ○ Mailing lists and personal information
- ○ Plants and seeds
- ○ Postage meters
- ○ Prescription drugs and devices
- ○ Recalled items
- ○ Satellite and cable TV descramblers
- ○ Stocks and other securities
- ○ Stolen property
- ○ Surveillance equipment
- ○ Tobacco
- ○ Travel

Questionable

These items may be listed under certain conditions. Do further research before putting your auction up to be sure your item is allowed.

- ○ Artifacts
- ○ Autographed items
- ○ Batteries
- ○ Catalytic converters and test pipes
- ○ Charity or fund-raising listings
- ○ Contracts and tickets
- ○ Electronics equipment
- ○ Event tickets
- ○ Food
- ○ Freon and other refrigerants
- ○ Hazardous materials
- ○ Imported and emission-noncompliant vehicles
- ○ International trading in any category that violates current laws

Is That Legal? (continued)

- ○ Manufacturers' coupons
- ○ Materials targeted to mature (adult) audiences
- ○ Offensive material
- ○ Pesticides
- ○ Police-related items
- ○ Presale listings (items that are not in the control or possession of the seller at the time of the listing)
- ○ Slot machines
- ○ Used airbags
- ○ Used clothing
- ○ Used medical devices
- ○ Weapons and knives

Potentially Infringing

These items may be in violation of certain copyrights, trademarks, or other rights. eBay prohibits some of these items, regardless of the particular item's legality, because they almost always violate copyright and trademark laws. As with questionable items, do your homework before posting your auction.

- ○ Academic software
- ○ Authenticity disclaimers
- ○ Beta software
- ○ Bootleg recordings
- ○ Celebrity material
- ○ Contracts and tickets
- ○ Downloadable media
- ○ Faces, names, and signatures
- ○ Items with misleading titles
- ○ Items that misuse another product's brand name
- ○ Mod chips, game enhancers, and boot discs
- ○ Movie prints
- ○ OEM software
- ○ Recordable media
- ○ Replica and counterfeit items
- ○ Unauthorized copies

Technical
Basics

Not long ago, one of the biggest challenges of online auctions was the complexity of using them. Fortunately, times change. Today, eBay is an incredibly user-friendly system, whether you're buying or selling.

Tip...

Smart Tip

Once your eBay account
is set up, spend some time—
at least several hours—browsing around, getting familiar
with the site and its abundance of features before you
begin buying and selling.

Longtime eBay seller Sue Rudolph recalls, "In the beginning, eBay was not user-friendly for sellers. It was easy to buy from, but hard to list on. And that intimidated me." Today, she says, you can easily learn to buy and sell on eBay, whether you're a computer novice or a computer nerd.

We're not going to spend time in this book walking you through the steps to register on eBay for two primary reasons. First, most people who are serious enough about learning to sell on eBay that they buy a book on the subject have already browsed the site and probably have already done a little buying and selling, so they already know how to register and use the site. Second, the eBay site itself will take you through the process quickly and efficiently. However, here's a piece of useful advice: If you happen to have a teenager in your home, as do many of the eBay sellers we talked with, just ask him or her to help you. Kids are a wealth of technological information.

If you haven't already registered on eBay, you should know that all registered eBay users are required to provide contact information—name, address, e-mail address, and telephone number—when they register, and must maintain valid and current information on file. If your contact information changes, be sure to notify eBay immediately. You will also need to provide a credit card number and your checking account information. eBay uses this information to confirm your identity and therefore protect the integrity of their operation, and to collect auction fees.

If you are unable or unwilling to give out your credit card and banking information, you can circumvent this process by becoming ID Verified. Many sellers choose to become ID Verified to prove they are trustworthy community members. To take advantage of this procedure, you must pay a small fee and supply personal information to eBay, including your name, date of birth, and details of certain credit accounts. This is not a credit check and will not affect your credit rating; it's just proving your identity beyond a shadow of a doubt.

eBay has strict rules about when user contact information is released. You can request contact information for eBay users who are involved in your current or recent transactions when that information is necessary to complete the transaction. For example, sellers can request contact information for all bidders in an active transaction and the winning bidder in a successful closed auction. Bidders can request contact information for a seller during an active transaction and if they are the winning bidder in a closed auction. Contact information may be useful if a bidder has a question about the item description and is unable to contact the seller by e-mail, if a seller needs information from a bidder to compute shipping charges or in some other way finalize the transaction, if a seller wants to verify the bidder by phone, or if a buyer or seller wants to resolve a listing-related dispute.

Your eBay User ID

Choose your eBay user ID thoughtfully. This is the name under which your reputation as a buyer and seller will be established. Though it's possible to change your user ID, it's not always a good idea. If you change your user ID, people who have done business with you before may not be able to find you by searching using your old user ID. One good thing about changing your user ID is this: Your history follows you, and your feedback remains intact, so any reputation you've worked hard to build will come with you no matter what your user ID is.

When choosing your user ID, consider the image it's likely to project to prospective customers. When Liz Baker first starting buying and selling on eBay, she was doing it for fun and therefore chose a whimsical user ID that reflected her love of animals: theditzydog. However, that name just didn't work well for a serious professional bidding on projects on Elance, so she created a different user ID to use for that. "If I had realized what a tremendous opportunity eBay offered, I would have chosen a more professional-sounding user ID from the start," she says. Since then she has changed her eBay user ID to more accurately portray her specialty in used books: theliterate-lady. Sellers are permitted to have more than one eBay account as long as their reasons

The Urge to Merge

e Bay allows you to combine several user IDs, including feedback scores and comments, into one. If you do this, the old user IDs are no longer active and can't be used. eBay allows you to merge a maximum of two old user IDs into one, and the newly combined user ID cannot be merged again.

According to eBay's policies, to request a merge, you must meet the following requirements:

- ❍ Be able to prove that you are the owner of the old and new user ID's. Generally, that means the contact information on your old user ID needs to match that of the new user ID.
- ❍ The old user ID must have no bidding or listing activity within the last 60 days.
- ❍ You must have confirmed registration of the old and new user IDs.
- ❍ The old user IDs must have a zero balance on the account; you cannot owe any seller fees on a user ID you merge.
- ❍ You must use the same billing currencies (such as dollars or pounds) on both the old and new user IDs.

are legitimate. However, there should never be any interaction between accounts belonging to the same person, especially in the areas of bidding and feedback.

Your user ID should also be easy to remember. A combination of letters and numbers that might make perfect sense to you (say, the first two letters of each of your children's names, followed by their birth months) could be hard-to-remember gibberish to someone else. Peggy Webb decided to use "wwwebbs" as her user ID because it seemed fitting to identify her brood as the "World Wide Webbs," while Susan Marler chose ozfreak2 because she has a passion for Wizard of Oz collectibles.

It's not uncommon for sellers to make mistakes with their original user IDs and want to change them later, but they may be reluctant because they don't want their customers to lose track of them. eBay has addressed this issue to a degree: Buyers who have marked you as a "favorite seller" will have your new name automatically updated on their My eBay page. Another drawback of changing your user ID is that you get a "name change" icon next to your new user ID for 30 days, and that could make some new potential buyers suspicious.

Doing Research on eBay

Before you start buying or selling on eBay, you should be comfortable doing searches (or research) on the site—so practice before you have any money at stake.

You can do a basic search from just about any page on eBay. On eBay's home page, you'll see a large yellow search box near the top of the page. By typing in specific keywords, you can search all of eBay's auctions or just those in a particular category. You will find a similar search bar on other pages that provide a listing of auctions to look at. On pages with auction descriptions, there also will be a small search box at the top right-hand corner of the page. When you type the search word or phrase for what you're looking for in that box, the system will check the titles of all currently open auctions and give you a list of matches.

For a more complete search, check the link immediately beside or underneath the search box that says "Advanced Search." This will give you the opportunity to look for keywords and phrases in the auction description, as well as in the title. You should also get comfortable doing more advanced searches, such as by item number, seller or bidder user ID, category, location, price range, and payment method.

When you run across sellers who are doing the type of business that interests you, study what they do by searching according to their user ID. Look at their current listings, review their completed auctions, study their About Me page and their eBay store, and figure out how to apply their successful techniques to your own operation.

Along the same lines, monitor the activities of buyers who are shopping for the types of goods you want to sell. Whom are they buying from? What are their bidding patterns? How much are they paying? What else are they buying that you might also want to sell? By clicking on their feedback number (the number in parentheses next to their user ID), you can see what other people have said about them and what they have said about other people, as well as some of the items they've recently bought or sold. When the feedback list comes up, it will include the item number of the auction; you can click on that number for details of what the merchandise was and what they paid for it. eBay keeps completed auctions clickable for a limited period of time, usually not more than two weeks.

Studying completed auctions can tell you a lot about what is happening on eBay. Looking at minimum bids and Buy It Now prices can give you an idea of what sellers would like to get for their merchandise, but studying completed auctions tells you what buyers were willing to pay. Some sellers believe it's the best way to find out what is going on in the eBay marketplace.

Smart Tip

Tip...

Smart Tip

Kevin Peterson, author of the CD-ROM *eBay Smart—Building a Real eBay Business by Going Beyond the Get-Rich-Quick Game* (SpinSmart Software), advises sellers to choose a business name with an available dotcom address so they can benefit from the synergy, or simply direct the dotcom to their eBay store. "If possible, make the name keyword-rich," Peterson says. "For instance, if you sell handbags, 'snazzy-handbags' is much more search engine–friendly than 'snazzydesigns.'"

While most items that are listed on eBay are eventually sold, not all of them do. That means looking at active auctions alone doesn't provide sufficient information to evaluate the selling potential of a particular item. You should be looking at bid history and final sale price of ended auctions. Just because something is listed doesn't mean there's a market for it.

Search Tips

Whether you're looking for something to buy or researching the market before putting an item up for sale, eBay offers these tips to help you find what you're looking for:

- *Try different search words.* Items can be described in a variety of ways. Imagine the words a seller might use to describe the item you're seeking, and try several different options and combinations. Use just two or three words at a time for the best results.

- *Be specific, not general, and if appropriate, specify date, color, or brand.* To get targeted results from a search, be precise with your phrasing. For example, "crystal vase" will get better results than simply "vase"; "Waterford crystal vase" refines the search even more.

- *Add or remove the letter "s" for more results.* For example, a search for "necklaces" produces different results than a search for "necklace."

- *Understand how to use "and," "or," and "the."* When you put those words into a search, eBay's search engine looks for them just as it does any other word, so use those words only if you're searching for items containing those words, such as "Gladys Knight and the Pips" or "Truth or Dare." To search for one word or phrase that would be used in combination with another word or phrase, learn eBay's search commands, which can be found through the Help function.

- *Watch your punctuation.* Use punctuation in your search only if you expect it to be in the item title or description.

- *Consider browsing.* Browsing the category listing pages is like going on a treasure hunt; you never know what you'll find.

- *Look for auctions that don't accept PayPal.* Since this is the preferred payment method for most buyers—and many buyers won't even consider a seller who doesn't accept PayPal—you can often purchase items at bargain prices and then resell them on eBay for a profit.

- *Look for auctions that have misspelled words in their titles.* Thousands of items are listed on eBay with misspelled words in titles. Because the majority of browsers search by keyword, these auctions are often overlooked and end without any bids. For example, at any given time you can find more than 1,000 listings that have misspelled the word "jewelry." "Labtops" can be purchased very inexpensively, as well as art "deko" objects and "daimond earrnigs." Think of commonly misspelled words or use the free toolbar found at www.misspellsearch.com.

- *Use wildcards to broaden your search.* An asterisk symbol (*) can be used as part of a keyword if you are looking for variations. For example, Baker frequently looks for vintage cookbooks to add to her collection. When conducting a search, she often types in "18* cookbook" to see what volumes are available from the 1800s. The search results can be as few as 10 listings or more than 50 on any given day.

- *Search descriptions as well as titles.* Sellers may not always include the keyword you are looking for in the title. By default, eBay searches for keywords in the auction title unless you specify otherwise. So another way to broaden your search is to click the "Search Title and Description" box found on search pages or under Advanced Search.

- *Narrow your search results.* If your keyword or phrase turns up too many listings, you can narrow the search results by placing a minus sign (-) in front of words that you don't want to show up. For example, if you are looking for a large plaid comforter (queen or king) and you don't want it to be part of a set, you could enter a search string like this: plaid comforter, -set, -pillow, -twin, -full. Keep excluding words until you have streamlined the search to your specifications.

- *Save your search.* If you have fine-tuned a search string that you will use again, save it in your "Favorite Searches" in My eBay. You can pull up the search results whenever you want without having to retype the information. You can also request that eBay send you daily e-mail notifications whenever auctions are listed that match your parameters.

Common eBay Icons

As you browse around eBay, you'll see an assortment of icons that can be very informative. Here are some of the more common icons and what they mean:

- *About Me.* A blue and red "me" after a user ID indicates that user has an About Me page with more information about his or her eBay operation, and serves as a link to the user's About Me page.

- *Buy It Now.* The Buy It Now icon means the item has a set price for which it can be purchased immediately without going through the bidding process.

- *Camera.* A camera means that a picture is included with the listing.

- *Change user ID.* Two people with an arrow between them is the "changed ID" icon and indicates a member who has changed his or her user ID within the last 30 days.

- *eBay store.* A red door next to a seller's ID indicates they also have an eBay store.

- *Gallery.* An icon with a small picture frame indicates that the item is featured in eBay's gallery. It means you can see the item's photo in search results and browse listings.

- *Gift services.* The neatly wrapped present icon means the seller wants to highlight the item as a potential gift that they will wrap and ship directly to the recipient.

- *Live auction.* An auction paddle means an item is part of eBay Live Auctions.

- *New!* The yellow "new" icon indicates a new service or feature on eBay.

- *New item.* A rising sun icon next to a listing indicates that the item has been listed within the past 24 hours. New item icons are automatically removed after the listing is 24 hours old.

- *New user ID.* A person with a sunburst behind their head indicates a new member. The icon alerts you that you might be dealing with a new eBay user who may need a little extra patience and assistance.

- *PayPal logo.* When you see the double "P" next to an auction listing, this means the seller accepts PayPal. If a checked shield is included in the logo, this indicates the transaction can be covered under PayPal's Buyer Protection Program.

- *PowerSeller.* A blue silhouette in a gold star next to the words PowerSeller indicates that this user has achieved a certain sales volume and performance status within eBay.

- *eBay Giving Works.* An icon featuring a blue-and-yellow ribbon means the seller is going to donate a portion of the proceeds from that auction to charity through eBay's Giving Works program. These are traditional auctions that appear in a typical eBay search, as well as in the charity listings.

- *Feedback stars.* Sellers are awarded different-colored stars when they achieve a certain feedback rating.

Abbreviation Station

As in any community, there's a "language" on eBay of common abbreviations used in auctions (especially in auction titles, where space is at a premium and character counts count!) and when buyers and sellers communicate. Here are some of the ones you'll need to know:

- ❍ *IBIN:* Buy It Now
- ❍ *ICOA:* Certificate of authenticity
- ❍ *IDJ:* Dust jacket
- ❍ *IFS:* Factory-sealed
- ❍ *IHB:* Hardback [book]
- ❍ *IHTF:* Hard to find
- ❍ *ILN:* Like new
- ❍ *IMIB:* Mint in box
- ❍ *IMIMB:* Mint in mint box
- ❍ *INARU:* Not a registered user
- ❍ *INBW:* Never been worn
- ❍ *INC:* No cover
- ❍ *INIB:* New in box
- ❍ *INIP:* New in package
- ❍ *INOS:* New old stock (old stock that hasn't been sold or used)
- ❍ *INPB:* Nonpaying bidder
- ❍ *INR:* No reserve
- ❍ *INWOT:* New without tags
- ❍ *INWT:* New with tags
- ❍ *IOOAK:* One of a kind
- ❍ *IOOP:* Out of print
- ❍ *IPB:* Paperback [book]
- ❍ *IRET:* Retired
- ❍ *ISH/S&H:* Shipping and handling
- ❍ *IVHTF:* Very hard to find

How to Sell on eBay

Selling on eBay is really very simple as long as you approach it systematically. The first step is, of course, to set up a seller's account. Then decide what payment forms you'll accept (see Chapter 9) and set up those accounts. Do this before you start listing items for sale.

Next, choose a selling format. The most popular is, of course, eBay's standard online auction format (Chapter 5 discusses this in greater detail), but you can also sell through your own eBay store (see Chapter 6) or set a fixed price for your item. Then select your category, write a great title and description, decide how long you want your listing to run, when it should start and end, what your minimum bid will be, and other pricing details, add pictures, enter your payment and shipping information, and then very carefully review your listing. If everything is accurate, submit your listing.

There are more ways than just this one to start an auction on eBay, and sellers who do more than a little bit of part-time selling on eBay usually use a bulk listing tool to start their auctions. This makes it possible to start multiple auctions at one time and streamlines the listing process. eBay provides two primary listing tools, Turbo Lister and Seller's Assistant, and these are discussed in depth in Chapter 7.

Beware!
In a traditional live auction, the auctioneer will keep accepting higher bids until the bidders stop bidding. An online auction ends at a particular time, so the bidding may be fast and furious in the closing minutes.

Most sellers monitor their auctions to see how many people are looking and how the bids are going. Prospective bidders may have questions about your item. eBay allows them to contact you via e-mail from the listing, and you should answer those questions as quickly and completely as possible.

Once your auction has ended, communicate with the winning bidder regarding payment, shipping instructions, and any other details that need to be handled. When you've received payment, ship promptly and leave feedback for the buyer. For more on feedback, read Chapter 7.

Learn the Language—HTML, That Is

Hypertext Markup Language, or HTML, is a simple programming language that is commonly used to create web pages. You can use HTML to jazz up your eBay listings.

By putting codes within the "less than" and "greater than" symbols (< and >), you can tell text how to appear in your listing. For example, inserting <b> before text will make that text bold—until you enter the command to end the bolding, which is </b>.

When HTML codes (also known as tags) are inserted in text, it can look confusing until you put the text up on eBay or on a web site, and the coding disappears but the text shows up with all the attributes you want. As you're creating your document, you may find it easier to work with if you add blank lines so you can see the coding more clearly. Those extra lines will be ignored when the HTML is interpreted.

eBay's site includes basic information about how to use HTML in your auction listings. You can also enter "HTML" in any search engine, and you'll find a wide range of online resources that will explain how to create HTML documents. Or look for premade auction templates that will convert your text to HTML, which can then be copied and pasted into eBay's listing description form. A list of free and fee-based sites featuring auction templates can be found in the "Auction Software and Support" section of the Appendix.

It's entirely up to you whether or not you use HTML in your auctions, and it's certainly not mandatory. Many eBay sellers use only simple text and photos in their auction listings, and they run profitable businesses. It's possible to go overboard with HTML, of course. Too many colors, too many fonts, too many different font sizes, etc., can get a little busy. Sometimes, the simpler an auction looks, the better.

Your Own Web Site

A web site lets you sell products to a potentially different market than you'll reach on eBay. You can put a link on your site to your About Me page on eBay (or put a link to your web page in all your auction listings), and some people may decide to skip the auction process and buy directly from you. You'll also attract internet shoppers who don't use eBay.

Unless you are extremely proficient with web design, hire a professional to put together an attractive, user-friendly site for you.

ProStores

Another way to create an online presence outside eBay is by using ProStores, a complete e-commerce solution for retailers. ProStores are stand-alone web sites that can be integrated with any eBay listing. These stores come with their own shopping carts, product catalogs, mer-

Bright Idea

Use your web site to take advantage of affiliate programs. This is when you put a link to someone else's site on your web site. If a visitor to your site clicks on that link and then joins the affiliate's program, you earn a commission. Be careful to choose affiliate programs that will be of interest to your target audience.

chant capabilities, and many other features that can be customized to suit your needs. ProStores are compatible with eBay, allowing you to easily create auction-formatted or fixed price listings on eBay whenever you want from your web site, or vice versa by copying eBay listings directly to your ProStore. Although sellers are responsible for marketing their stores, more customers will be driven to these stores, thanks to eBay's search engine optimization. If you have a lot of products and want to have an off-eBay store in addition to a presence on eBay, this is a convenient way to do it and have everything tied together.

Auction Management Software

While it's possible to have a profitable business selling on eBay without using any additional software, good auction management software will save you time and money, make you more efficient, and improve the level of customer service you offer. "It's very easy to learn eBay," says Gotham City Online's Jonathan Garriss. "It's very easy to sell an item on eBay. It's very difficult to do that efficiently." Supplemental software helps automate your processes to improve productivity and profitability. Auction management software is also helpful if you use other online auction sites in addition to eBay.

With an eBay business, most sellers get to a certain point where they are unable to manage the auction process manually. Fortunately, there are many automated tools and software programs that can help you do everything from listing the items and handling the billing to posting feedback and paying fees.

Of the eBay sellers we spoke with, the smaller volume ones tend to do things manually or use eBay's tools, while the larger volume ones use auction management software or have developed their own systems to manage their operation. Georgene Harkness of My New Threads uses Spare Dollar (www.sparedollar.com) to list and manage all her auctions. "I like it because I can schedule the auctions to go up whenever I want," she says. "Plus, they have all sorts of custom templates. It's very convenient and easy to use."

David Lynn of CRI says he started out using eBay's tools but eventually upgraded to Channel Advisor (www.channeladvisor.com), which provides auction management software and services. "Once the sales started growing, the time for processing all the shipments was way too much to do without a good management platform," Lynn says. "It's pricey, but we feel paying for expensive software is cheaper than hiring one or two additional people to process the orders."

Tip...

Smart Tip

Once you've mastered the basics of operating on eBay, begin exploring options and tools to make you more efficient and profitable, and increase your volume.

▲

You can purchase software or subscribe to an online service that will help you create your listings, launch them manually or automatically at the time you determine, manage your photographs, count how often your listing is viewed, send e-mails to buyers, manage inventory, print shipping labels, post feedback, and more. Some auction management service providers also offer payment processing. Auction management software will also provide you with reports that will help you manage your business more efficiently.

Whether you decide to use eBay's auction management tools or third-party services, the important thing is to streamline your business and make it as automated as possible so that you can concentrate on your customers and making them happy.

5

eBay Auctions
The Foundation
of eBay Selling

To put something "up for auction" on eBay is not complicated or difficult—however, it's not quite as simple as those three words might sound. The online auction world is not a one-size-fits-all proposition. Under the broad category of auctions falls a variety of types, and you need to choose the one or ones that will get the best results for you and your particular

▲

Smart Tip

Use eBay's completed search function to study completed auctions for items similar to what you want to sell. You can see the bid patterns, photograph quality, listing style, and other elements, and then determine what works best and use those ideas for your own merchandise. Go to the general search function on eBay, click on "Advanced Search" or "Smart Search," and then select "Completed Items" under "Display" on the left-hand side of the page.

products. As you're getting started, you may want to do some experimenting with the different types of eBay auctions to see how they work.

Traditional auctions are the backbone of eBay and can run for one, three, five, seven, or ten days. The auction begins with an opening bid, and when the time is up, it closes with the highest bidder winning. This is a very easy process; however, depending on your business strategy and the type of product you are selling, you may want to think about using other types of auction formats.

Reserve Price Auction

Auctions that have a hidden minimum price are known as reserve price auctions. The reserve price is the lowest amount the seller is willing to accept for the item. Buyers are not shown what the reserve price is; they only see that there is a reserve price, and whether or not it has been met. If the reserve price is not met, the seller is not obligated to sell the item. To win the auction, a bidder must meet or exceed the reserve price and have the highest bid.

In a reserve price auction, bids are made as usual, but bidders receive a notice if their bid does not meet the reserve price. Once the reserve is met, the item will sell to the highest bidder when the auction closes.

Sellers see reserve pricing as a way to protect their investment without revealing up front how much they want to get for the item. Liz Baker has occasionally used reserve prices and says they've always been met. But many bidders avoid reserve auctions because they can't tell what the lowest winning bid needs to be, and they don't want to waste their time bidding on an item that may have a high reserve figure.

Andrew Robinson of Boston Tables in Columbus, Ohio, says they sometimes use reserve auctions in competitive climates and when they want to list items at low starting prices. "If we use a reserve auction, we typically want a lot of eyeballs to look at that auction," he says. "We then put enough written text in the description so that a customer will be enticed to look at our other auctions or visit our store." Robinson says the reserve price is usually met and the item is sold, but their main goal for using reserve auctions is to encourage people to look at their other listings.

Buy It Now

This is a feature you can add to a traditional auction format that gives bidders the option to bid on your product or to buy it immediately. With Buy It Now, you set the price you're willing to sell for, and bidders can either place a bid for less than that amount (but at or above your starting price) or win the auction instantly by paying the Buy It Now amount. When a bidder agrees to the Buy It Now price, the auction ends. If someone places a bid below the Buy It Now price, the Buy It Now option disappears.

Here's how it works: Let's say you post an item with a Buy It Now price of $15 and an opening bid of $3. If someone is willing to pay $15 and there are no other bids, the auction is over as soon as that person agrees to buy the item for $15. Or, someone can bid $3, the Buy It Now option goes away, and the auction proceeds like any other auction. That $3 might be the only bid you'll get, or bidding could drive the final sale price above $15.

Georgene Harkness of My New Threads likes the Buy It Now feature and says it has been a big moneymaker for her by bringing sales to a fast conclusion—especially during the holidays, when people are in a hurry to get the item. "When I set a BIN, I imagine the highest price I think the item will sell for and add a 'fantasy' bonus of 20 percent," she says. "I've made a lot of money doing that."

A good strategy used by many sellers is to start the bidding at the absolute minimum you will accept for the item and then set the BIN amount close to full retail. If you get anything in between, you've made a profit and the customer is happy with their bargain.

Fixed Price Listings

Technically, a fixed price listing is not an auction because there is no bidding, but those listings show up in auction search results. This format allows users to buy and sell items immediately at a set price, with no bidding or waiting. You can sell more than one item in a fixed price listing, which saves you time and money in listing fees.

Private Auctions

In most auction formats, anyone looking at the item can see the user IDs of the people who are bidding on it. With the private auction format, however, the bidders' user IDs are not seen on the item or bidding history screens. When the auction is over, only the seller and winning bidder are notified via e-mail.

This format is useful when you believe your prospective bidders may not want their identities disclosed to the general public. Well-known collectors often prefer private auctions. A common use of this format is for collectibles when just the knowledge that a certain collector is bidding on an item would greatly increase the interest in the auction. Private auctions are also appropriate for items not intended for mass viewing, such as adult material.

Dutch Auctions

When a seller offers two or more identical items for sale in the same auction, it's known as a Dutch (or multiple item) auction. There can be many winners in this type of auction. For sellers, the power of a Dutch auction is that it allows you to sell large quantities of a single item with just one listing.

When you post a Dutch auction, you decide on your minimum bid amount (the lowest price you're willing to accept) and list that along with the total number of identical items you have available. Bidders specify the number of items they're interested in and the highest price they're willing to pay per item.

Beware!

You can't bid on your own auction, but if you change your mind about selling your item before the auction ends, you can cancel all bids and end the auction early. Once the auction ends with a bidder, you are contractually obligated to complete the sale.

What makes Dutch auctions interesting—and complicated—is that all winning bidders pay the same price per item, which is the lowest successful bid. Most commonly, all buyers pay the starting price. But if there are more bids than items, the items will go to the earliest successful bids at the close of the auction. Bidders may bid on any quantity but have the right to refuse partial quantities.

Here's how it works: You have 50 toy airplanes you're willing to sell for $5 each, but if you could get more, you'd be pleased. So instead of listing 50 separate auctions (which would also mean 50 separate listing fees, and you'd have to space those auctions out over a period of time because of eBay's restrictions on the number of simultaneous auctions for identical items) or a fixed price auction (which would eliminate the possibility of the items selling for more than your starting price), you put the toy airplanes up as a Dutch auction with a starting price of $5 each.

If 50 people bid $5 on one airplane each, then at the close of the auction, those 50 people would be the winning high bidders, and each would receive one toy airplane for the price of $5.

But Dutch auctions aren't always that simple. If any one of those people had bid more than $5, everyone would still only have to pay $5. For the final price to be more than $5, all the winning bidders would have had to bid more than the starting amount. So if 100 people placed individual bids on those toy airplanes, and 20 of those bids were for $8, 30 were for $7, 15 were for $6, and the remaining 35 were for $5, the toy airplanes would be sold to the first 50 bidders for $7 each, because that was the lowest successful bid. The lowest successful bid was $7 and not $5 because there are only 50 airplanes and 100 bidders. You start counting back from the highest bid until you reach the number of bids

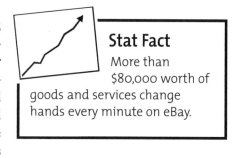

that matches the number of items; then everyone pays that bid price.

Here's another possible scenario: Let's say Sam bid on 25 of the toy airplanes at $5 each, then Mary bid on 10 of the airplanes at $5 each, George bid on 10 of them at $6 each, Cathy bid on 10 at $5 each, and Harry bid on 5 at $5. Even though George bid $6, all the toy airplanes will be sold for $5 each, because that was the lowest successful bid. So Sam will get his 25, Mary will get her 10, George will get his 10, but there are only 5 left for Cathy. Cathy has the option to accept the 5, but she can also refuse them because she wanted 10. If Cathy refuses the 5, the seller can then go to Harry to complete the sale.

Bidders in Dutch auctions do not receive outbid notices from eBay, nor can they use eBay's proxy bidding system (which allows a bidder to enter a hidden maximum bid), so they must actively monitor the auction and rebid if necessary.

The most important things to keep in mind when using the Dutch auction format are that the items in a single Dutch auction must be absolutely identical, and the auction itself must be listed in the appropriate category.

Don't be tempted to try something known as "Dutch avoidance"—that is, listing a single item and offering additional identical items for sale in the item description. Sellers who do this typically instruct buyers to indicate the number of items they want and offer those items at the same price as the item in the listing. Sellers who successfully do this manage to avoid paying the full final value fee (see below) for everything they sell, but the practice is dishonest and against eBay policy. Listings that violate this guideline will be ended by eBay.

Live Auctions

This particular type of auction is of more interest to an online buyer rather than a seller, but it's something you should know about. eBay's live auctions feature allows you to bid real time on auctions that are happening on the floor of offline auction events. You can place absentee bids, bid against the floor or just watch the auction—all from the convenience of your home or office. For more information, go to www.ebayliveauctions.com.

Restricted-Access Auctions

This category makes it easy for buyers and sellers to find or avoid adult-only merchandise. To sell, view, and bid on adult-only items, users must have a credit card on file with eBay. Items listed in the adult-only category are not included on eBay's New Items page or the Hot Items section, nor are they available by any title search. Failure to list an adult-only item in the correct area could result in a suspension.

eBay's policies stipulate that all users must abide by all applicable regulations regarding the sale and distribution of adult materials, and any violation of the law is also a violation of eBay's user agreement, and will be treated accordingly.

Want It Now

This is a type of classified ads section where buyers can post requests for specific items and sellers are able to respond with matching eBay listings. This free service enables sellers to expand their market by looking for buyers for items they have on hand. Buyers can search by category or keywords. They can also save searches to be used again and elect to receive alerts on corresponding Want It Now (WIN) requests. Once you, as a seller, have determined that you have a matching item, you can send an e-mail to the buyer through eBay with a link to your listing. One out of two WIN bids results in a successful transaction.

Best Offer

As a seller, you can allow prospective buyers to make an offer on your listing; however, these auctions need to be set up as a fixed price format. Many buyers search specifically for auctions that have a "Submit Best Offer" feature, so this can be an additional marketing tool for you. Best Offers are binding, and all messages relating to the transaction must be conducted through eBay and not violate any trading policies. Buyers are only allowed to make one offer per listing, so if you decline a bid, the buyer cannot come back and try to haggle with you. This is to encourage people to seriously make their best offer at the outset. You will receive an e-mail notifying you when a Best Offer has been made, and you have 48 hours to respond before the offer expires, so check your messages for other offers often.

Auction Fees

While eBay is free to buyers, sellers must pay to use the site. The pricing structure is very similar to traditional auctions, although the amounts are very modest. The different types of fees are explained here, but eBay periodically adjusts its fee structure, so you should check the site for the current fee amounts.

Insertion Fees

You must pay a nonrefundable insertion fee or listing fee for listing your item on eBay. This fee will vary with the type of listing.

- *Single quantity, online auction listings.* The insertion fee is based on the minimum bid you set for your item—the lower your minimum bid, the lower the fee.

- *Reserve price auction listings.* The insertion fee is based on the reserve price of your item—as with the minimum bid, the lower your reserve price, the lower the fee. You will also be charged a reserve price auction fee, which is refunded if your item sells.

- *Dutch auctions and multiple item fixed price listings.* The insertion fee is based on the opening value (the minimum bid or the fixed item price multiplied by the quantity of items) of your merchandise.

Final Value Fees

When your item sells, eBay will charge a final value fee based on the final sale price. For regular and reserve price auctions where the reserve price is met, the final value fee is determined by the winning bid. For Dutch auctions, the final value fee is determined by multiplying the lowest successful bid by the number of items sold. For multiple item fixed price listings, the final value fee is calculated by multiplying the Buy It Now price by the quantity of items sold.

For general merchandise listings, the final value fee is a percentage that drops as the closing value increases. For vehicles and real estate, the final value fee is a flat amount.

A final value fee is not charged if there were no bids on your item, or if you listed a reserve price auction and the reserve price was not met, and therefore the item did not sell. But if you have bids on the item, and those bids meet your reserve price if you had one, you will be charged a final value fee whether or not the buyer pays for the item and completes the transaction.

> **Bright Idea**
>
> Watch for eBay listing specials. Periodically eBay will offer steep discounts on various listing features to encourage you to try them. (Sometimes eBay charges only a penny to use the Gallery feature, when it normally costs 35 cents.) Take advantage of these money-saving offers.

If something goes wrong after the auction ends and the sale doesn't go through, you can request a refund of your final value fee. The circumstances under which eBay will consider issuing a credit for the final value fee include if the buyer didn't pay or if the buyer paid but returned the merchandise and you issued a refund.

▲

Listing Upgrade Fees

eBay offers sellers a variety of ways to promote their merchandise through listing upgrades. The fees vary from a nominal amount (as low as 5 cents) to substantial (approximately $100 or more, if you combine features) and are nonrefundable.

Listing upgrade features include:

- *Home Page Featured.* Your listing will be featured on eBay's home page, as well as on its special Featured Items page.

- *Featured Plus!* Your listing will be seen at the top of search results pages, as well as in general listings.

- *Highlight.* You can have your listing placed in a brightly colored box that will stand out in search results.

- *Bold.* Your auction title will be displayed in search results in a boldface font.

- *Gallery.* A photo of your item will show up next to the listing when it appears in search results.

- *Gallery Featured.* An enlarged photo of your item will appear in the featured section of the Gallery View.

- *List in Two Categories.* Listing your item simultaneously in two different categories doubles its exposure to browsers.

- *Ten-Day Duration.* This keeps your auction listing open longer for more browsers to see it.

- *Scheduled Listings.* Using this feature, you can schedule listings to launch up to three weeks in advance.

- *Buy It Now.* This gives buyers the opportunity to purchase your item immediately without waiting for the auction to end.

- *Gift Services.* This lets buyers know that your item would make a great gift for which you can offer gift-wrapping, cards, and shipping alternatives.

- *Listing Designer.* This feature provides a variety of templates and layouts to help you create professional auction listings.

- *Item Subtitle.* This appears underneath the title in search results and includes additional information about your item.

- *Border.* A purple border will appear around your listing title when it appears in search results.

- *Picture Services.* To post and showcase more than one picture using eBay's service, use this feature.

See "Marketing Your Auctions" on page 59 for more information on how to use these listing upgrade features to enhance your auctions and increase your income.

PayPal Fees

PayPal is an eBay service that provides a fast, easy, secure way for people to exchange funds online. There is no charge to open a PayPal account or to make payments using PayPal. Payments can be made by withdrawing money from deposits made to your PayPal account, by withdrawing money from your own bank account through PayPal, or by using a credit card through PayPal. Personal accounts are free but cannot accept credit card payments. eBay sellers who offer PayPal as a payment option are required

> **Bright Idea**
>
> Before you list, find out what else is on the market and how it will affect your listing. When Sue Rudolph sells an antique or a collectible, she doesn't want a dozen other items like it up for auction at the same time. For example, she checked eBay before she listed a Royal Doulton Princess Diana doll, and the same doll was already listed. She listed her doll after the other auction closed.

to upgrade to a Premier or Business account so buyers have the ability to pay with a credit card. With Premier and Business accounts, you are charged a fee to receive funds. Fees are assessed at the time of the transaction.

Timing Is Everything

Experienced bidders often wait until the final hours or minutes of an auction to bid to avoid driving the price up too early. Those final hours are also the time when auction fever can strike, with bidders in fast and furious competition over who is going to purchase your items. This is why you need to keep timing in mind when you put your auctions up.

The most popular online shopping days are Saturday, Sunday, and Monday, and the least popular are Thursday and Friday. Time your auctions to end on one of those popular shopping days to maximize bidding activity. eBay offers auctions with one-, three-, five-, seven-, and ten-day durations. eBay seller Buz Moran prefers five-day auctions. "You get a quicker return. Start it on Tuesday and it ends on Sunday," he says.

If you're using ten-day auctions, list them so they cover two weekends, which gives you the benefit of high weekend traffic twice.

Capture late bids by scheduling your listings to close at hours that are convenient for your target market. Close auctions for consumer items and collectibles during evening hours, when more individuals are likely to be online shopping and bidding. For items that are more appealing to a business or dealer, close your auction during normal work hours.

Robinson recommends that sellers have at least one auction within the category they are representing expiring every day of the week. The reason, he says, is that people usually pull up their searches by items that are either recently listed or currently expiring. "We try to get listings that expire between 10 and 11 P.M. [Eastern Standard Time] so the West Coast is already at home, too," he says. "And depending on seasonality, we'll frequently have an auction a day expire around lunch time, when a lot of people check their computers."

The eBay Scheduler lets you choose the day and time your auctions begin, so you can prepare your listings at your convenience and still have an optimum close date and time. There is an extra charge for using this service. Other auction software programs will do the same thing.

Getting Your Auction Listed on eBay

There's a very logical sequence to getting an auction posted on eBay. Learn how to do it manually before you graduate to automated systems. Start by choosing your listing type from the options we've discussed. If you're unsure, consider what types other successful sellers have used for similar products.

Determine Your Starting Price

This is the lowest price you're willing to accept for your item (unless you have specified a reserve price), and this is the amount at which bidding starts. Be reasonable when calculating this figure. Certainly you want to make a profit on what you sell, but sellers have found that setting the starting price too high often discourages bidding. A lower starting amount may attract a flurry of initial bidders who will quickly drive the price up. If you are using a fixed price format, you'll enter a Buy It Now price. See the pricing section in Chapter 9 for tips on how to determine your starting price.

Write Your Title

eBay allows 55 characters (letters and spaces) for your listing's title, and you need to make each one count. Your title must make a prospective bidder want to learn more about your auction.

It helps if your headline is clever and catchy, but above all, it must be accurate and factual. Tricking people into looking at your auction because they think it's something else won't get you more bids—but it will make people mad, and they'll remember that the next time they look at one of your auctions. Also, misleading titles are against eBay policy and could result in eBay ending your auction early. Though you might see them often, devices such as "L@@K" and excessive exclamation points don't attract additional bidders, but they do brand you as an amateur. Use all caps sparingly and only to make certain words stand out.

Beware!
If the item you are selling is related to a particular event, such as tickets for a performance or a holiday, be sure your auction closes in time to allow shipment to the buyer.

Your title needs to include the keywords that someone who is looking for your item might conduct a search for. If you have room, include a related word so your listing will come up in more searches. For example, let's say you're selling a pair of candleholders. Your title could read "Stunning Antique Cut-Glass Candleholders." Not bad, but if you wrote "Cut-Glass Candleholders For Tapers, Candles," you would come up in searches for cut glass, candleholders, tapers, and candles in general. Certainly if someone is searching for the size or style of candles that your candleholders accommodate, they might be interested in another pair of candleholders, even if they weren't initially searching for them. So be creative in the language you use in your titles. Think of everything your item relates to, and figure out how you might be able to get as many of those words as possible into your title.

Your title should also indicate why your listing is special. Consultant Paul Mladjenovic uses a picture of Frank Sinatra as an example. Let's say you have a photograph you believe will appeal to people who collect Sinatra memorabilia. The headline "Frank Sinatra Photograph" will probably get some hits. But "Rare Photo: Frank Sinatra At Last Concert" will probably attract more interest from serious collectors. However, use the word *rare* sparingly and only when truly accurate. It's a commonly overused term in eBay auctions and sometimes means it's the only item of this kind the seller has in his possession at the moment.

If you are selling a brand-name item, include the brand name in the title. However, do not compare brand names in your title; only include the brand of the item you are offering. If the item is clothing or something that comes in different sizes, indicate the size.

Write Your Description

Investing time in writing a good description will pay off in the price you receive. A well-crafted description gives bidders the information they need to make a buying decision, as well as demonstrates that you are a professional, conscientious seller. A sloppy, incomplete description will not inspire confidence in prospective bidders. You need to tell what you are selling clearly, completely, and using powerful, persuasive words. Look at your items as though you have never seen them before and know nothing about them. Then write a description that will make someone want to own what you're selling.

Your description should include:

- the name of the item;
- what the item is made of;
- when and where it was made;
- who made it (company, artist, designer, author, etc.);
- what condition it's in;
- weight, size, and/or dimensions;
- notable features or markings; and
- any special background or history.

Everything in your description should be true and accurate. If an item is damaged or missing parts, don't say something vague, such as "easily restored." If possible, identify exactly what needs to be replaced, or suggest the buyer purchase the item to be used as parts for another piece. You might also add a personal touch to your description; many sellers have found that doing so can increase bids and sales. For example, specifically say what you like about the item, whom it would appeal to and why, and how it could be used. If you know an interesting story about the item, share it. For example, you may have an antique silver spoon that was once owned by Henry VIII. You'll probably get a decent price if you just describe it as an "antique silver spoon," but add the detail about its previous owner, and the value increases.

If the item is not in perfect condition, be honest. Describe any scratches, chips, stains, and other imperfections. Failing to do this can create a disgruntled customer and result in negative feedback and perhaps returned merchandise.

Although bidders can e-mail you using a link on your listing page if they have any questions, don't assume you'll hear from them if they want more information. Though some will write, many will just bid on something else that's described better.

Beware!
While it's good to model your own eBay operation after those of successful sellers, don't use another user's images or descriptions in your listings or About Me page without that user's permission.

Think about how you would react to short and obviously incomplete descriptions. A bid is a contract—are you willing to make a commitment to buy something you don't know much about? Do you wonder if the seller is trying to hide something?

Something else to keep in mind as you write your description is not to do something known as "keyword spamming," which is against eBay's listing policies. This means you shouldn't include words in your description that are not actually related to your item just because you think buyers would find those words appealing and because they are words a search would pick up. For example, don't write, "This dress is an Anne Klein style," unless it really is an Anne Klein design.

At the same time, use as many legitimate search words and phrases in your description as possible so your item will come up when bidders are searching.

You can also use your description to add details about shipping costs, payment terms, and any other details you think may be of interest to a bidder. Georgene Harkness prefers to charge her customers a flat fee and state that amount in the auction description. "My customers seem to like it better when they don't have to figure out how much the postage is going to be or wait for an e-mail confirmation," she says.

Even if you plan to charge actual shipping, it's always a good idea to include at least an estimate of the shipping costs so bidders aren't surprised when the auction is over. For example, since the post office charges by weight and distance, you can calculate the postage to a nearby ZIP code, and then to one far away, and write in your description: "Buyer pays actual postage. Estimated cost will be $5 to $8 via USPS parcel post (5 days) or $7 to $12 via Priority Mail (2 to 3 days)." Also, let bidders know if there are any restrictions on where you will ship, such as U.S. only, U.S. and Canada only, or to certain international locations. eBay has a shipping calculator that you can insert in your auctions that allows the buyer to determine how much it will cost to mail that item to their address via USPS or UPS.

When you're finished, proofread and spell check—and then proofread again.

Choose the Right Category

With millions of items up for sale at any given moment on eBay, putting your auction in the correct category is essential. While many bidders will do searches looking for specific items, others just browse categories looking for any item that interests them. One of the biggest mistakes unsuccessful eBay sellers make is listing in the wrong category.

Browse around eBay and find items that are similar to what you want to sell, and see what categories they're listed in. Check completed auctions to see what the final sale price was, and look for trends that would indicate that listing an item in one particular category gets better results than another.

Marketing Your Auctions

eBay offers a wide range of services you can use to market your auctions. Some are free; most are available for a nominal fee.

A featured auction is given extra exposure in the "Featured" sections at the top of the listings pages. Andrew Robinson says he likes to run featured auctions several times a week for Boston Tables. Although the cost may sometimes eat up a significant amount of profit on that particular item, the exposure attracts buyers to other nonfeatured auctions and generates substantial revenues that way. It's an approach very similar to the loss leaders you see in grocery stores—when popular items are sold at cost or below just to get people into the store.

The Gallery feature places a photo along with your title in search results. This allows viewers to see your item without having to click on the full listing. An attractive gallery photo will make your listing stand out. Jonathan Garriss says gallery images have worked well for Gotham City Online, and David Lynn says all his company's auctions are gallery listings. Single mom Laurie Ayers says they are well worth the extra charge because they "grab attention." And eBay says listings with gallery photos get a lot more bids than those without gallery photos.

Robinson says subtitles are well worth the small additional fee because they quickly catch a browser's eye when your listing shows up in a search. "We can also put

Feature Presentation?

When writing up your auction listings and product descriptions for items in your eBay store, pay attention to the difference between features and benefits. "Benefits are what people will derive from a product, and features are just telling you the nuts and bolts description of the product," says consultant Paul Mladjenovic. Don't just list a product's features; be sure to include the benefits as well.

For example, the features of a multivitamin are its ingredients; the benefits are that you will feel better, live longer, be healthier, or whatever. The features of a set of dishes include the color, the material, and the pattern; the benefits may be that your dinner table will look elegant or that, because the dishes are very durable and will stand up to rough treatment, you'll save money by not having to replace them soon.

You must list features because those are the facts about your items. Just be sure that for every feature, you list at least one corresponding benefit.

Fine Crystal

White with Blue Stripe

Very Durable

more keywords in a subtitle and have found them to be a better investment than many of the other features," he says. However, be aware that subtitles will not be picked up in a traditional keyword search unless the buyer has checked the "Search Title and Description" box.

If you think your item would make a good gift, use eBay's gift services feature. The gift icon (a wrapped package) will appear next to your listing on search and browse pages and tells buyers if you offer gift services such as gift wrap, gift cards, express shipping, and shipping directly to the gift recipient. Your item description should include details of and charges for the gift services you provide.

You can also dress up your listing with highlighted and bold text in the headline, and you may want to list your item in two different categories for additional exposure.

In addition to promoting your auctions within the eBay community, consider using your own personal or professional network as well. If you belong to a club or have friends who share a common interest and you are selling something that may appeal to that group, let them know about it. Set up an automatic signature on your e-mail that includes a notice about your auctions at the end of every message you send.

When you post your auctions, make your listings sparkle by adding bold, italics, and color to your text. Use HTML, which was discussed in Chapter 4; take advantage of one of the many different types of auction templates available online; or use eBay's Listing Designer tool. But be cautious when adding features that include motion and sound. For users with dial-up connections, these listings can take a long time to load, and some bidders may opt to move on to another listing rather than wait. Also, while sound may be cute and possibly even entertaining, it could end up being a tattletale feature if someone is browsing around eBay when they should be doing something else (like working). Moran says, "My philosophy is to keep it simple and quick."

The Bidding Process

For most auctions, the bidding process is fairly straightforward. You set your minimum bid, and people interested in buying your merchandise place successively higher bids until the auction closes. Beyond that, however, are some details about bidding you need to know.

Proxy Bidding

eBay's proxy bidding system allows buyers to enter the maximum amount they're willing to pay for an item, then sit back and relax while the computer handles the bidding. It works this way: When placing a bid, bidders enter the highest amount they're willing to pay for the item. This number is kept confidential from other bidders and

▲

Bright Idea

If your item is unique, spe-
cialized, or requires buyer
research, use a ten-day auction so
bidders have plenty of time to check
it out and decide how much to bid.

the seller until the auction ends. The eBay system places bids on behalf of the bidder, using only as much of the bid as is necessary to maintain the high bid position or to meet the seller's reserve price. The system will bid up to the bidder's maximum amount.

If another bidder has a higher maximum, the first bidder will be outbid and will receive an outbid notice. At that point, a bidder can go back and rebid or choose to let the item go.

In reserve price auctions, if a bidder's maximum bid is the first to be greater than the seller's reserve price, the eBay system automatically makes a bid that meets the reserve, and the bidding process continues from there.

The drawback for sellers is that even though someone may be willing to pay more for an item, the proxy bidding system will only take the bid up to the next increment required to win the auction. But it's a benefit to buyers, because it means bidders often end up paying less than their maximum price.

Proxy bidding does not apply to multiple item (Dutch) auctions.

High-Dollar Bids

When placing a bid of $15,000 or more on eBay, users are required to provide a valid credit card or go through eBay's ID verification process. This assures sellers that the bidder is of legal age and serious about completing the transaction.

Bid Retractions

All bids on eBay are binding except those involving the sale of real estate or businesses (which fall under eBay's nonbinding bid policy) and the sale of items that are prohibited by law or by eBay's user agreement.

Though eBay rarely allows users to retract their bids, there are some circumstances when it is permitted. Whether you are selling or buying, it's important to understand the rules about bid retractions.

One such situation would be if the bidder accidentally enters the wrong amount—for example, if a bidder enters $550 instead of $55. In that case, the bidder must re-enter the correct bid amount immediately after making the retraction. If the bidder doesn't place another bid, he is in violation of eBay's policy and may face suspension.

A bid can also be retracted if the description of the item being auctioned is changed significantly after the bid is made but before the auction closes. Bids can also be retracted if the buyer cannot reach the seller by phone or e-mail (for example, if

Let the Bidding Begin

The bid increment, or amount by which a bid is raised each time the previous bid is topped, is predetermined based on the current high bid. However, it's possible for a bidder to be outbid by less than a full increment. This would happen when the winning bidder's maximum bid beats the next highest bid by an amount less than the full increment. eBay bid increments are:

Current Price	Bid Increment
$ .01–.99	$.05
$1.00–4.99	$.25
$5.00–24.99	$.50
$25.00–99.99	$1.00
$100.00–249.99	$2.00
$250.00–499.99	$5.00
$500.00–999.99	$10.00
$1,000.00–2,499.99	$25.00
$2,500.00–4,999.99	$50.00
$5,000.00 and up	$100.00

the seller's phone number on file with eBay doesn't work or if e-mail messages are returned as undeliverable).

Bids placed before the final 12 hours of a listing may be retracted if they meet one of the above circumstances but only if the retraction is made prior to the final 12 hours of the auction. A bidder who retracts a bid under these circumstances eliminates all bids he has placed on that item, so if the retraction is to correct a bidding error, a new bid must be placed.

For bids placed during the final 12 hours of a listing, retractions must be made within one hour of placing the bid and are allowed only if the situation meets eBay's rules. If a retraction is made within the last 12 hours, only that particular bid will be eliminated; bids placed prior to the last 12 hours will remain valid.

Of course, bidders may contact the seller and request that a bid be canceled, and the seller may honor the request or not at his own discretion.

Every user's feedback profile displays the total number of bid retractions that user has made in the past six months. Be cautious about accepting bids from a user who has a habit of retracting them. Also, eBay investigates bid retractions, and users who abuse this feature may be suspended.

▲

It's important to note that there is no equivalent for a bid retraction in Buy It Now listings. Once a purchase has been confirmed, the buyer is obligated to pay.

Sniping

Sniping is the process of placing bids in the closing minutes or seconds of an auction. Snipers do this to avoid bidding wars that escalate the bids to more than they want to pay. Bidders can protect themselves against snipers by bidding the absolute maximum amount they are willing to pay with eBay's proxy bidding system. A sniper—or any other bidder—can only win the auction if they are willing to spend more than anyone else who has bid. When a last-second bid isn't high enough, that person rarely has time to get back in and place a winning bid before the auction ends.

Because eBay is a global marketplace and listings end at all hours of the day and night, serious snipers use programs that will place their last-minute bids for them. A handful of these services are free, but most have a fee that users insist is well worth it.

A Picture Really Is Worth 1,000 Words

eBay automatically adds the camera icon to listings with pictures so someone browsing through search results knows when they click on your listing they'll be able to see what the product looks like.

While any picture is better—albeit only slightly—than no picture at all, a quality picture will make a tremendous difference in the success of your auctions. Quality photos not only let bidders see what your product really looks like, but they also say that you're a serious, professional eBay seller. Antiques seller Sue Rudolph says you'll get more and higher bids on items when your pictures are good.

Use the following tips to produce quality photos that will increase bidding on your auctions:

- Create a photo area in your home or shop with a background screen and good lighting. Cluttered backgrounds detract from your product and brand you as an amateur. Poor lighting will prevent prospective bidders from seeing the detail they need to make a decision about if and how much to bid. Georgene Harkness uses a 500-watt halogen light on a stand that also has two smaller bulbs as fill-in lights for lighting purposes.

- For small items, a sheet of plain poster board makes a good neutral backdrop.
- Consider developing a photo background that helps brand your business. It

> **Beware!**
> As a seller, you may cancel the bid of any user with whom you feel uncomfortable completing a transaction.

could be a distinctive (but not distracting) color, it may have a subtle pattern, or it could include your logo or company name.

- If appropriate, showcase your item with accessories to display it to its best advantage. Accessories should not distract from or hide any details of your products. Also, be sure to indicate whether or not those accessories are included in the auction, available separately, or not for sale.

Relist Me

If an item doesn't sell the first time you list it, try relisting it with a lower minimum bid. If it sells the second time around, you'll be credited for the insertion fee for the second listing. (Of course, if it doesn't sell the second time, you'll pay the fees for both listings.)

eBay makes this relisting offer under the following conditions:

- ○ You did not receive any bids if your listing was a regular, no-reserve auction; or, if your listing was a reserve price auction, you did not get any bids that met or exceeded your reserve price.
- ○ You are relisting the same item within 30 days of the closing date of the first listing.
- ○ You have the same or lower starting price than the first listing for a no-reserve auction, or for a reserve price auction, you relist with the same or lower reserve amount.
- ○ The transaction resulted in an Unpaid Item, where the buyer defaulted on payment.

eBay allows one free relisting per item and unlimited paid relistings; check eBay's policies for complete instructions and restrictions on this offer. When you relist, consider writing a different title, changing the starting price, enhancing your description, or changing or adding photos.

- If you sell clothing or jewelry, invest in used mannequins to properly display your merchandise. A box draped with a piece of plain fabric works as a display pedestal.

Garriss says photography is one of the biggest cost issues for eBay sellers. He recommends maintaining a database of pictures so it's easy to pull up images for listings when you are selling items you've sold before. "We have a library of about 350,000 images that we are able to tap when we have the same items come through again," he says.

Most eBay sellers find the investment in a digital camera worthwhile, but it needs to be a quality camera. Moran started out using print film that he would have transferred to a disk when it was processed, but that, he says, took too long. Then he received a good-quality digital camera as a gift and is now able to take clear pictures that showcase his items well.

If you have a scanner, you can use print film and then scan your photos. Or, if you have an image of the product from a catalog, you can scan that instead of staging a new photo—just take care not to violate any copyright restrictions.

And remember: If you're in the market for a good digital camera and/or a scanner, shop on eBay first.

Once you have the pictures uploaded to your computer, you can use software to adjust and enhance your images. Many digital cameras come with their own software that allows you to crop, brighten, and fine-tune photos. You can also find online software—sometimes free—that can eliminate blemishes such as speckles or lens dust, as well as tweak the color. Harkness uses several programs that help improve the quality of her pictures. "Sometimes the halogen lamp turns things a little pink, so I use Picasa2 (http://picasa.google.com/index.html) from Google to adjust the color," she says.

Check the Appendix to find other photo editing programs.

6

eBay Stores
An Easy Way to
Sell Online

Along with putting merchandise up for auction on eBay, you may want to consider opening an eBay store, which would allow you to sell your fixed price and auction items from a unique destination on eBay. eBay stores make it easy to cross-sell your inventory and build repeat business.

If your goal is a small, part-time operation selling just a few items a month, an eBay store might be helpful, but not necessary. However, if you want to build a substantial, profitable business, you may want to consider opening an eBay store. It's an excellent tool.

How do you make the decision? According to eBay, you should open an eBay store if you want all your listings displayed in one customizable place, if you want to be able to easily generate repeat business and encourage multiple purchases from the same buyers, if you want to control what you cross-sell to your customers, and if you want to maintain a larger permanent inventory than what you sell through auctions.

eBay stores offer a convenient selling platform for all your eBay listings—auctions, fixed price items, and store inventory. eBay promotes stores in several ways. All your auction listings will contain the eBay store icon; when bidders click on that

Level with Me

eBay offers three store levels: basic, featured, and anchor. All have their own customizable storefront and the ability to list store inventory, but featured and anchor stores include additional services. Check the eBay web site for current store subscription fees. Here's how the three levels differ from one another:

- ○ *Basic.* Your store is automatically listed in the eBay stores directory and will appear in every category directory where you have items listed.
- ○ *Featured.* Your store rotates through a special featured section on the eBay stores home page, receives priority placement in "related stores" on search and listings pages, and is featured within the category directory pages where you have items listed. In addition, you receive monthly reports on your sales and marketplace performance.
- ○ *Anchor.* In addition to the services offered to featured stores, your store can be showcased with your logo within the eBay stores directory pages and will receive premium placement in "related stores" on search and listings pages, which means your store will be placed higher on the page than the featured stores.

Peggy Webb uses her store, Pages-and-More, as her main site. "The listings are less expensive, so that is where I keep most of my stock," she says. "But every so often, I will drag out something and put it on auction as a vehicle to get people to come to my store." David Lynn also uses auctions as a type of loss leader for his Combined Direct store to attract visitors.

icon, they are taken to your store. That icon is also attached to your eBay user ID for increased visibility. The eBay store directory is designed to promote all stores and will drive buyers to your particular store. You will also receive your own personalized eBay store web site address that you can distribute and publicize as you wish.

The process of opening an eBay store is almost as simple as setting up your initial user ID. The only requirements are that you be a registered eBay seller and have a minimum feedback rating of 20 or be ID-verified.

Any items that you have in active listings at the time you open your store will not appear in your store. But any auctions or fixed priced listings you post once your store is opened will automatically appear in your eBay store.

The cost of a basic eBay store is a nominal monthly fee (current rates can be found at www.ebay.com) that increases with the level of services you desire, along with additional fees for items listed and sold. Store inventory listings are less expensive than auction listings and appear for a longer time. However, those listings appear only in your store and do not come up in traditional eBay auction searches.

In addition to insertion fees, as with auctions, you also pay final value fees when an item in a store listing sells.

Setting Up Your Store

Just as you would stock a physical store using a well-thought-out arrangement of your merchandise, you want to apply the same principles to your eBay store. eBay allows you to create up to 20 custom categories for your products. Use these like aisles in a physical store, grouping like products together under a clear description to make it easy for shoppers to see what you have.

Depending on what you sell, you may decide to use product-based categories, such as clothing, home decor, glassware, electronics, etc. Or you might use a more flexible system, with categories like "sale items," "bestsellers," and "seasonal." Consider having a category for new items so people who visit your store regularly can quickly see what you've added recently. These custom categories can be changed and updated as often as you wish, which is a significant benefit to a seller whose inventory changes frequently.

Your store site should also clearly explain how you operate. Take advantage

Bright Idea

Successful store sellers use their auctions to drive traffic to their stores. Kevin Peterson, author of *eBay Smart: Building a Real eBay Business by Going Beyond the Get-Rich-Quick Game* (SpinSmart Software), says eBay stores are not good stand-alone vehicles. "To draw people to your store," he says, "you need to post auctions and reference the store in them."

of the Store Policies page to provide a complete and professional description of your policies and procedures. Your About My Store page tells customers about your business and works the same way your About Me page does (discussed in Chapter 7). Use this space to establish your credentials and provide some history about you and your company. Buyers are more comfortable dealing with sellers who demonstrate that they know what they're doing.

Be sure to use your store to list all the items you have in your inventory that complement your active auctions, and be sure to mention your store in all your eBay listings.

Remember that good descriptions and titles as well as clear pictures of the merchandise in your eBay store are as critical as they are in your auction listings.

Do You Want Fries with That?

You probably can't count how often you as a customer have been the target of up-selling efforts. Order a sandwich and drink at a fast-food restaurant, and you can bet you'll hear the familiar "do you want fries with that?" question. Displays at the checkout counters of retail stores are designed to persuade you to purchase something you didn't realize you needed. Call the customer service department of most major companies, and you're not surprised when the rep tries to sell you an additional product or service after dealing with the original reason for your call. It's all based on the economic reality that subsequent sales to the same customer are more profitable than the first. And when customers are in a buying mood, you should take advantage of it.

Smart Tip

Include your eBay store's URL in all e-mail communication with buyers. For example, add a standard line such as "Thank you for shopping with us. We add new products every week. Please visit us at www.ebaystores.com/storename."

All stores have the advantage of strategically placing promotional boxes on different pages that can be used to highlight featured items, provide special announcements, or be used in a variety of ways to showcase your store.

You also get cross-promotion tools that help you upsell by allowing you to control which items your buyers see after they bid on or buy one of your items, or use the checkout function after a transaction has ended. You can choose different items to show on each listing. For example, if you're selling candleholders, show buyers the candles, lighters, snuffers, and wax remover. If you're selling clothing, show the accessories such as shoes, scarves, hats, and jewelry. If you're selling home decor or furnishings, show complementary pieces.

The tools work by allowing you to establish "merchandising relationships" for the items you list, and this determines which items the buyers will be shown. You determine what goes together by designating relationships for as many or as few items as you'd like. If you don't include cross-merchandise on one of your items, eBay will automatically select related items you are selling to display to your buyers.

Jonathan Garriss of New York City–based Gotham City Online recommends that sellers provide plenty of cross-sell links to other items shoppers may like and offer a carrot to buy that additional item, such as free shipping. "We provide a number of quick links that help our customers find things," Garriss says. "Since we sell mostly shoes, a buyer may see a pair of shoes they love but need in a different size. So we provide easy links for that."

No Need to Physically Stock Your Store

It's possible for you to carry items in your eBay store that you don't already own and will never actually take possession of. It can work this way: You find a distributor of products you want to sell. You put photographs and a description of those products on your store site. Note that you don't have to sell everything the distributor does. When an order comes in, you process the payment (retail price plus shipping), and then send the order to the distributor, who ships the product directly to your customer in a package that shows you as the shipper. The distributor bills you the wholesale price plus shipping and handling. You make a profit, the distributor makes a profit, and the customer is happy and comes back to buy more—it really is that simple.

This is what is known as drop-shipping, and it is a long-standing business practice. It's win-win: You don't have to stock inventory, handle the product, pack, ship, etc., and the distributor doesn't have to worry about retail sales. Although Boston Tables imports a significant amount of their own merchandise, Columbus, Ohio, company owner Andrew Robinson says they also add to their selection with drop-shipping programs.

Of course, you have to choose the right merchandise and deal with reputable distributors. Your customer will give you the credit for what goes right and hold you responsible for what goes wrong, even though the drop-shipper is doing the work. You should also expect to pay for the services the drop-shipper provides. That will usually appear as a drop-ship fee, but it may be included in the cost of the merchandise. Be sure you understand how the drop-shipper charges so you can build that expense into your pricing structure.

Avoid drop-shippers who want to charge an account setup fee or insist on a minimum monthly purchase. Be sure that they are factory-authorized wholesalers of the brands they represent, and that the goods they are shipping

 Beware!
Do your research on your suppliers so you can avoid getting involved in a broker "daisy chain" (a chain of brokers who are each marking up the products). There is nothing wrong with buying from brokers or distributors, but you should always know who the actual seller is and be able to contact the seller directly if necessary.

are brand-new, factory-warranted products. Go back and review the information in Chapter 3 about buying from wholesalers before you commit to a drop-shipping arrangement.

While it may sound as easy as 1-2-3 to shoot an order over to the manufacturer—who will package and ship the product while you collect the proceeds—this process has its flaws, and sometimes they are too numerous to deal with long term. For example, a customer may receive goods that were damaged during shipping and look to you for restitution. You then file a claim with the manufacturer, who blames the carrier for careless shipping, who blames the manufacturer for inadequate packing, and nobody is happy—especially the customer, who might file a claim against you and post negative feedback. For these reasons, you may decide it's more advantageous to be a hands-on kind of seller and take care of packing and shipping yourself.

Be Prepared for the Commitment

One of the challenges of brick-and-mortar retailing is the hours—usually long, going from early morning to late evening, weekdays and weekends. Physical stores need to be staffed at least from opening to closing, and usually before and after.

By contrast, your eBay store is open for business 24/7, whether you're awake or asleep. But this doesn't mean you can put up a store and then ignore it. You need to monitor your store closely, answer questions from shoppers promptly, ship merchandise on schedule and as promised, and deal with any other customer service issues that might arise as soon as possible.

If you go on vacation or are going to be away from your store for any reason, you can either arrange for someone else to monitor the site and take care of your business, or you can place your store "on vacation" for an indefinite period. However, you will continue to be charged the normal store subscription and listing fees.

7

eBay
Tools

Your online image is a critical element in your success on eBay. It doesn't necessarily have to be slick and high-powered, but it does have to inspire confidence in bidders. Having a professional look to your auctions and your store (if you have one) is a major part of your online image.

If you've done any browsing around eBay at all (and by now, you should have), you can tell just by looking at an auction whether or not the seller is serious about his or her business. In Chapter 5, we discussed the importance of well-written, complete listings that have been carefully spell checked and proofread. eBay offers a variety of other tools to help you enhance your auctions, as well as your other eBay activities. Some are free, and some have a fee. To help you decide which tools will help you the most, eBay has a wizard (found under "Seller Tools") that offers tool recommendations.

About Me Page

Your About Me page is a great way to educate bidders on what you have to offer, your policies (payment terms, shipping, returns), and why they should feel comfortable buying from you. eBay provides a number of design templates to help you quickly design a sharp, professional-looking About Me page. Before you set yours up, browse around and look at others through the eyes of a prospective customer. Take the time to formulate your policies and write appealing copy that a prospective customer will read and understand.

In some ways, your About Me page is like a jazzy resume, but instead of using it as a tool with which you apply for a job, you're using it as a tool to win the confidence and trust of potential customers. Include information about yourself, such as details on your expertise in your product areas or business experience. You might also add a photo, but make it relevant to your eBay operation. It could show you at work doing something related to your business or even just be a professional-style headshot. Many successful eBay sellers include personal details on their About Me pages, such as information about their family or hobbies. While this shouldn't be the focus of your About Me page—this isn't, after all, your personal web site—it's still true that when bidders know something about you and feel like they can relate to you, your sales will go up.

Peggy Webb uses her warm-and-friendly About Me page to introduce people to the Disabled Online Users Association (DOUA) and tell a little about her disability. "Somewhere in my auction description I put that I'm a member of the DOUA, and for more information, go to my About Me page," she explains. "This way, the organization is getting exposure and people can learn what it's about and how it can help others." Webb says her About Me page has been a great educational tool because she has sent several disabled customers who previously knew nothing about the organization to the DOUA site.

You can also include a link to your personal web site on your About Me page; however, you cannot offer non-eBay merchandise for sale on your About Me page.

My eBay

My eBay is a tool that allows you to manage your buying, selling, and other account activities. Tustin, California, part-time eBay seller Linda Parker says this is her favorite eBay feature—and the page she visits most—because it allows her to track her own auctions plus what she's bidding on, her favorite sellers, and items she's just watching or searching for.

The tabs on the My eBay page are:

- *Bidding/watching.* This is the page where you track your bids, purchases, and the items you're interested in but haven't bid on (this is called watching an auction). You can create customized searches and be notified by e-mail when an item that fits your description is put up for auction on eBay. While this is

> **Tip...**
>
> **Smart Tip**
> Save all your auction listings in your word processing program or in your auction management software so that if you sell a similar item, you don't have to re-create the listing.

obviously a benefit to buyers, Sue Rudolph of Winter Park, Florida's Sweet Sue's Antiques and Appraisals says it also comes in handy for sellers to monitor their markets and to possibly buy items they might later resell.

- *Selling.* This is the page that shows all your auction listings, sales, unsold items, and pending items (listings you've prepared but haven't launched yet). From this section, you can generate mailing labels, invoices and reminder notices. Although Plano, Texas–based Georgene Harkness uses a third-party auction management software system for listing purposes, she does all her invoicing through My eBay because it is so convenient.

- *Favorites.* This page lets you keep track of what's going on in your favorite categories, searches, and with other eBay sellers.

- *Accounts.* All of your eBay-related accounts are in one place.

- *Feedback.* This lets you view the feedback you've received from other users. There is also a button that takes you to a list of the transactions for which you still need to leave feedback. Liz Baker in Oviedo, Florida, appreciates this particular feature. "It's easy to get busy and forget to leave feedback, but feedback is a very important part of the eBay community," she says. "I periodically use this tab to see if I have any transactions that are completed that I need to leave feedback on."

- *Preferences.* This lets you control how your My eBay page appears, how you prefer to sign in, and other eBay preferences.

- *All.* This combines all the information in all the tabs on a single page.

▲

Turbo Lister

Turbo Lister is a feature-rich eBay selling tool that makes creating and posting listings in bulk faster and easier. There is no charge to use Turbo Lister, but you have to download the Turbo Lister program from eBay and install it on your computer. (Go to http://pages.ebay.com/turbo_lister/, or request a CD from eBay.) The program helps you create auction listings in bulk, allows you to save listing details for items that you sell regularly so you can list them again later, saves default values for all "Sell Your Item" options to reduce data entry time, lets you duplicate items to make it easy to create listings for similar items, creates attractive item descriptions using a WYSIWYG (what you see is what you get) HTML editor, and schedules your listings to start at a specified time if you so desire.

Seller Central

Seller Central is the main hub where sellers can find the latest tips, resources, tools, and information on how to help their eBay business grow.

○ *Getting Started.* This area covers the basics of selling on eBay, from submitting a perfect listing to accepting online payments. There are plenty of resources for individual sellers, small-business owners, and corporations.

○ *Best Practices.* Here, you will find tried-and-true strategies to make your business successful. Learn how to research and price items competitively while selecting the bestselling format for your product. You can also find out which tools will give you the most exposure, as well as learn how to calculate shipping costs and track delivery of items.

○ *Advanced Selling.* Once you've mastered the basics of selling, you'll be ready to move into the next phase and discover how to track and analyze sales reports, use eBay keywords as a marketing tool, open an eBay store, or become a PowerSeller or Trading Assistant.

○ *Category Tips.* Gain a competitive edge by learning category-specific strategies and resources from successful sellers who know how to maximize their sales and profits.

○ *What's Hot.* Stay on top of the hottest trends and latest promotions on eBay. Here, you can find out what items are searched for most often and other little-known eBay facts.

○ *News & Updates.* Sign up for the monthly "Power-up" e-mail that provides information about upcoming events and promotions.

○ *Resources.* This is where you can find links to all the selling solutions on eBay.

Andrew Robinson of Boston Tables in Columbus, Ohio, says Turbo Lister is his preferred auction manager because it keeps everything concise and is easy to manage. "eBay frequently has updates, so I prefer to use their product," he says. "Third-party software may not be fully integrated with the most recent changes, and eBay is not going to support those flaws."

Selling Manager and Selling Manager Pro

These sales management tools can be accessed online through My eBay without downloading anything and are available for a small monthly fee; there is an exception for eBay store owners, who automatically receive the basic Selling Manager version for free as part of their store subscription. Selling Manager includes tools that help you organize and keep track of eBay sales, while Selling Manager Pro goes a step further by enabling you to create listings as well as track and manage your inventory and sales. Selling Manager Pro also helps automate the listing and postsale process. These tools can be used in conjunction with other eBay tools, including Turbo Lister.

Webb started using Selling Manager because she received a free subscription when she opened her store and found it to be a big help. She says that Selling Manager was much easier to access online than other auction tools that required a download and did not integrate well with her Mac computer.

Bidder Management Tools

Certainly one of the main benefits of selling on eBay is getting your goods out there in front of millions of prospective buyers. Even so, there may be times when you want to control who can bid on your auctions. eBay offers two tools for this purpose.

The first is your blocked bidder/buyer list. This allows you to set up a list of bidders/buyers who are not allowed to bid on or purchase your auction listings, and it applies to all the items you have up for any type of auction. You can add to or delete from this list at any time.

This feature can be used when you have a bad experience with a bidder, such as one who doesn't pay, takes a long time to pay, or who is unrealistic in his or her expectations and demands, and you simply don't want to do business with that person again. eBay suggests using this feature cautiously, as it may limit the number of bids on your items.

Rudolph had a bad experience with a bidder who had excessive negative feedback, so now, as her auctions near their closing time, she checks out the high bidder. If that individual has a lot

> **Tip...**
>
> **Smart Tip**
> In addition to eBay's tools, consider using other auction management tools, such as the ones available from the companies listed in this book's Appendix.

Beware!
You are never obligated to accept a bid from someone you don't want to sell to. You can refuse to do business with any eBay user for any reason, but you must cancel the bid before your auction ends.

of negative feedback, Rudolph sends an e-mail advising that she will not sell to that person and suggesting that he or she stop bidding on the item.

A more effective way to handle such a situation is to cancel the bid yourself and then place the bidder on your blocked bidder list. Here's how: Click on the "Site Map" link located at the top of most eBay pages; when that page opens, click on "Cancel Bids on My Item," which is located under the "Buying and Selling" heading near the top of the middle column. Follow the instructions for canceling the bid. You can also cancel a bid by going to the item's bid history page and clicking on the "Cancellation" link.

Once you've canceled the bid, add the bidder to your blocked bidder list so they can't bid on any of your auctions. Be sure to cancel the bid before you add the bidder to your blocked bidder list, or he may end up as the high bidder even though you've blocked him from future bids. As a courtesy, send a polite e-mail to the bidder advising that you've canceled the bid and explaining your reasons.

You may also create a preapproved bidder/buyer list for any item. This allows only the people on that list to bid on or purchase your auction items. If an eBay user not on the list sees the item and tries to place a bid, she will be asked to contact you by e-mail. You can add or delete bidders from your preapproved list up until the time the auction ends.

This is a useful tool when you want to sell something to a particular bidder but do not want to open the auction up to the public. For example, let's say you put up an item with a reserve price of $100, and the reserve was not met so the auction closed without a sale. Someone who saw the auction contacts you and offers you $95 for the item, and you decide to accept. It is against eBay policy for you to complete this transaction outside eBay. The easiest way for you to handle the situation is to relist the item with a starting bid of $95 and create a preapproved bidder list that includes only the user ID of the bidder you have agreed to sell to.

Second-Chance Offer

Although most eBay auctions are completed without any problems, occasionally a sale doesn't go through (usually because of a nonpaying bidder). Also, sellers often have duplicate items but only put one up for auction at a time. The second-chance offer is a feature that allows sellers to offer an item to an underbidder at the under-bidder's highest bid if the winning bidder does not complete the purchase or if the seller has more than one item available.

In the case of a nonpaying bidder, be sure you've done everything possible to resolve the issue before sending a second-chance offer.

As the name implies, a second-chance offer is an opportunity for the seller to sell the item (or another one like it) quickly and easily, with all the benefits of eBay's services, and without paying a listing fee. Sellers do, however, pay a final value fee if the second-chance offer is accepted.

eBay Education

eBay offers a wide range of narrated how-to "tours" to help users learn to use the system, as well as interactive written tutorials, online seminars, and recorded events.

The eBay University program offers a range of classes held across the country that allow you to learn in a traditional setting where you can interact with instructors and other students. The program includes one-track seminars, which are a day of classes that begin in the morning with basic topics and progress to more advanced subjects in the afternoon; two-track seminars, which are an entire day of either beginner or advanced training, depending on your needs; and road show seminars, which are shorter classes taught in different neighborhoods throughout a metropolitan area over a three-day period. Additional conferences and opportunities for learning and networking are available; check the eBay site for more information.

Feedback

Feedback is the tool by which an eBay user's reputation is built and is a large part of an eBay seller's success. eBay users leave 2.7 billion (and growing) feedback comments annually. There are three types of feedback—positive, neutral, and negative—and both parties in a transaction are encouraged to leave feedback about each other. For example, as a seller, you might leave feedback about how quickly a buyer paid; as a buyer, you might leave comments about how well the seller answered questions or how promptly the merchandise was shipped. Only the seller and the winning bidder can leave feedback about a particular transaction.

What you write in feedback becomes a permanent part of that user's record on eBay, so use caution and good judgment, especially before leaving negative comments. You cannot change feedback once it's been posted. And only in rare circumstances will eBay remove feedback after it is left.

An eBay user's feedback rating is the number in parentheses after his or her user ID. The feedback rating is calculated by giving one point for each positive comment, no points for a neutral comment, and subtracting one point for each negative comment. You should always check a user's profile for negative feedback, whether you're buying or selling.

Don't automatically refuse to deal with an eBay user who has a few negative feedback comments. Consider the ratio of negative feedback to positive feedback. If a user

Bright Idea

Use your feedback profile to boost your morale when you're having a bad day. Lift your spirits by reading all the positive things people have said about you.

has hundreds of transactions on his or her record, don't let two negative remarks dissuade you from doing business with that person. Also, look at when the negative feedback was left—recently, or a long time ago? Read the feedback and get a sense of whether it was justified or not, or possibly retaliatory because the other eBay member involved in the transaction left negative feedback for that person. Many of the negative feedback comments sellers receive are in retaliation for negative feedback the sellers leave for nonpaying bidders. So be sure to read all negative feedback comments—and decide for yourself if they're valid.

David Lynn of San Diego–based CRI says his company's eBay feedback is very good, with the exception of a few negative comments they received from newcomers a while back. "These seemed to be people who were not familiar with how eBay works and didn't use the feedback system as it was intended," he says. "For instance, one buyer stated that he didn't want to pay with PayPal and another complained that he wasn't going to order from us if we didn't have something else he wanted in stock." Anyone else reading these comments would know the buyers didn't actually have a bad experience with this seller; they just had different expectations or misunderstood the process.

If someone leaves you negative feedback, you can respond to the comments—and you should so that others can hear your side of the story. Just remember that this will be a matter of public record, so keep the facts simple and accurate, while remaining calm and professional. Something to the effect of "This is retaliatory feedback from a nonpaying bidder" or "Buyer refused refund" might be sufficient.

You should leave feedback within 90 days of the completion of a transaction. Of course, the sooner, the better. As you're building your own eBay reputation, you'll gain a special appreciation for users who leave prompt feedback.

Under certain circumstances, eBay allows both parties in a transaction (buyer and seller) to withdraw feedback after it has been left. This usually occurs when one or both parties prematurely leave negative feedback and then, if the transaction is resolved to both parties' satisfaction, they decide they want to remove the ding from the other user's feedback score. The feedback comment will still appear in your member profile with a note under it indicating that buyer and seller mutually agreed to withdraw the feedback, but it will no longer count in your feedback score. In other words, eBay doesn't deduct one point from your score for withdrawn negative feedback. Both members must agree, and feedback left by both parties will be withdrawn at the same time.

Warranty Services

If you sell electronics and computer items, you can increase your bidders' comfort level by offering a standard or extended warranty through eBay's Warranty Services program. You promote the warranty option in your listing, and a third-party company handles the warranty sale and servicing. For every warranty that is sold on one of your items, you earn a cash bonus of 25 or 50 percent of your eBay final value fee.

The general product categories for which warranties are available are computers, consumer electronics, cameras and photo, video games, and musical instruments. The item can be new, used, or refurbished, but it must be fully functional.

Due to state laws, sellers in Alaska, Guam, Maine, Oklahoma, and Puerto Rico cannot participate in the warranty program.

PowerSeller Program

eBay's PowerSeller Program is designed to recognize certain levels of achievement by eBay sellers. Because PowerSellers are held to strict standards regarding both their sales volume and their business conduct, Georgene Harkness (also a PowerSeller) says that customers are able to buy from sellers with confidence when they see the PowerSeller logo. In addition, PowerSellers have access to special benefits, such as the health insurance opportunity explained in Chapter 8.

eBay's system automatically assesses users for PowerSeller eligibility and issues an e-mail invitation to join the program when a seller qualifies.

> **Tip...**
>
> **Smart Tip**
>
> Andale Inc. provides counters to eBay sellers at no extra charge, and various other auction management programs will also count the number of times your listing is viewed. This is a good tool to use since it lets you know how popular an item is and whether or not your auction marketing efforts are working.

eBay's Certified Provider Program

This program was established to give eBay users access to a network of technical and nontechnical solution and service providers. This includes customized software development and auction strategies, such as template designs and product sourcing. To take part in the program, Certified Providers are carefully screened, must pass certification exams, and must have extensive experience serving the eBay community. Certified Providers are listed in the Certified Provider Catalog found by clicking the program's link on the eBay site map. Only these members can include the prestigious

Certified Provider logo in their marketing materials so eBay sellers can feel more comfortable using their services as they grow their businesses.

eBay Toolbar

This free, customizable tool is downloaded to your desktop and provides direct links to preferred eBay pages. It has a handy search box for quick results and sends you alerts on auctions you are watching, bidding on, or selling. Perhaps one of its best features is the Account Guard protection that lets you know when you are on a potentially fraudulent web site, while simultaneously protecting your account information.

Structuring
Your Business

If your only goal with an eBay business is to periodically clear out the garage and occasionally make a few extra dollars, your business structure doesn't really matter much. But if you're using eBay to launch a substantial and sustainable operation, you need to set it up right from the beginning.

Put It in Writing

Some entrepreneurs will do just about anything to avoid sitting down and writing a business plan. Other would-be business owners get so caught up planning every detail that they never actually get their business off the ground. Ideally, you should find a happy medium between these two extremes.

Gotham City Online's Jonathan Garriss says eBay offers so many different opportunities that a written business plan is essential to help you focus. You may see ten or more opportunities but, he says, "If you go in ten different directions, you're not going to make a lot of progress. You [probably] don't have the resources to pursue that many opportunities. Just doing the business plan is the exercise that defines where the best opportunity is and where you are going to commit your resources."

In a perfect world, you would begin your venture with a written business plan. Writing your plans down forces you to think them through and gives you a chance to examine them for consistency and thoroughness. That's why even if you're already buying and selling on eBay and have achieved a degree of success, you need a plan.

If you're excited about your business, creating a business plan should be an exciting process. It will help you define and evaluate the overall feasibility of your concept, clarify your goals, and determine what you'll need for start-up and long-term operations.

> **Tip...**
>
> **Smart Tip**
>
> Review your business plan once a year. Check to see if you're still on track—if not, do you need to change what you're doing, change the plan, or both?

This is a living, breathing document that will provide you with a roadmap for your company. You'll use it as a guide, referring to it regularly as you work through the start-up process and during the ongoing operation of your business. And if you're going to be seeking outside financing, either in the form of loans or investors, your business plan will be the tool that convinces funding sources of your venture's worth.

Putting together a business plan is not a linear process, although the final product may look that way. As you work through it, you'll likely find yourself jumping from equipment requirements to cash flow forecasts to staffing, then back to cash flow, on to marketing, and back to equipment requirements. Take your time developing your plan; whether you want to start a part-time solo eBay business that never gets any larger or build a sizable operation, you're making a serious commitment, and you shouldn't rush into it.

This book focuses on issues particular to selling on eBay, but there are additional points you need to consider when writing your plan.

Naming Your Company

One of the most important marketing tools you will ever have is your company's name. A well-chosen name can work very hard for you; an ineffective name means you have to work much harder at marketing your company.

Your company name should very clearly identify what you do in a way that will appeal to your target market. It should be short, catchy, and memorable. It should also be easy to pronounce and spell—people who can't say your company name may buy from you, but they might not tell anyone else about you.

We asked eBay sellers how they came up with their company names. Garriss came up with the name Gotham City Online because of his New York City location. He also made sure the corresponding web address was available before making the final decision. David Lynn said his company wanted its eBay business name to be closely aligned with its wholesale company, CRI (Combined Resources International)—hence the name Combined Direct. Bob Willey sells a variety of unique and interesting items, so he decided to call his company Bob's Neat Stuff because it was descriptive and catchy—plus, he has some really neat stuff!

It's important to think ahead about which direction you want your company to grow in and what impact your business name will have on it. You don't want to choose a generic or indistinctive name that you may eventually tire of or regret. If that happens, it may be too late to change it since you will have already created a brand for yourself that customers, suppliers, and the industry recognize.

Bright Idea
When naming your company, consider creating a word that doesn't exist—that's what companies like Exxon and Kodak did. Just be sure the syllables blend to make an ear-appealing sound and that the name is simple enough for people to remember. Also, check to make sure you haven't inadvertently come up with a name that means something with negative connotations in another language.

Although naming your company is undoubtedly a creative process, it helps to take a systematic approach to the task. Once you've decided on a name, or perhaps two or three possibilities, take the following steps:

- *Check the name for effectiveness and functionality.* Does it quickly and easily convey what you do? Is it easy to say and spell? Is it memorable in a positive way? Ask several of your friends and associates to serve as a focus group to help you evaluate the name's impact.

- *Search for potential conflicts.* Find out if any other business has a name so similar that yours might confuse the public.

- *Check for legal availability.* Exactly how you do this depends on the legal structure you choose. Typically, sole proprietorships and partnerships operating under a name other than that of the owner(s) are required by the county, city, or state to register their fictitious name. Even if it's not required, it's a good idea, because that means no one else can use that name. To find out how to register a fictitious name in your state, start by calling the local business licensing agency; they'll either be able to tell you or refer you to the correct agency. Corporations usually operate under their corporate name. In either case, you need to check with the appropriate regulatory agency to be sure the name you choose is available.

- *Check for use on the internet.* If someone else is already using your name as a site on the internet, consider coming up with something else. Even if you have no intention of developing a web site of your own, the use could be confusing to your customers.

- *Check to see if the name conflicts with any name listed on your state's trademark register.* Your state's department of commerce can help you obtain this register or direct you to the correct agency. You should also check with the trademark register maintained by the U.S. Patent and Trademark Office (PTO). Visit the PTO web site at www.uspto.gov for more information.

Once the name you've chosen passes these tests, you need to protect it by registering it with the appropriate state agency; again, your state's department of commerce can help you with this. Because you'll be doing business nationally, and perhaps even internationally, on eBay, you should also register the name with the PTO.

Legal Structure

One of the first decisions you'll need to make about your new business is the legal structure of your company. This is an important decision that can affect your financial liability, the amount of taxes you pay, and the degree of control you have over the company, as well as your ability to raise money, attract investors, and ultimately sell the business. However, legal structure shouldn't be confused with operating structure. The legal structure is the ownership structure (defining who owns the company). The operating structure defines who makes management decisions and runs the company.

A sole proprietorship is owned by the proprietor, a partnership is owned by the partners, and a corporation is owned by the shareholders. Sole proprietorships and partnerships can be operated however the owners choose. In a corporation, the shareholders typically elect directors, who in turn elect officers, who then employ other people to run and work in the company. But it's entirely possible for a corporation to have only one shareholder and to essentially function as a sole proprietorship. In any case, how you plan to operate the company should not be a major factor in your choice of legal structures.

So what goes into choosing a legal structure? The first point is who is making the decision on the legal structure. If you're starting the company by yourself, you don't need to take anyone else's preferences into consideration. But if there are multiple people involved, you need to consider how you're going to relate to each other in the business, as well as the issue of asset protection and limiting your financial liability in the event things don't go well.

Something else to think about is your target customers and what their perception will be of your structure. While it's not necessarily true, there is a tendency to believe that the legal form of a business has some relationship to the sophistication of the owners, with the sole proprietor as the least and the corporation as the most sophisticated. If you're going to be selling primarily to private consumers and collectors, they'll probably never know (or care) whether you're a sole proprietor or a corporation. If, on the other hand, your target market is going to be other businesses or high-end retail buyers, it might enhance your image if you incorporate.

Your image notwithstanding, the biggest advantage of forming a corporation is in the area of asset protection, which is the process of making sure that the assets you

Learning Curve

If you understand mail order businesses, you'll have a head start with your online auction business. And if you don't, it's a good idea to learn because the two operations have a lot in common, says consultant Paul Mladjenovic. Among those similarities are that you need to find customers and build relationships without the advantage of face-to-face interaction, you need to find merchandise, and you need to create a fulfillment (shipping) system.

Mladjenovic cites two primary differences between online auctions and mail order: "The first difference is irregular inventory," he says. Mail order houses typically have a standard stock that they ship out when ordered, while online auction sellers may have less predictable resources, especially if their product line includes collectibles and used merchandise.

The second difference is the method of pricing. "Auction businesses use dynamic pricing, while mail order businesses use static pricing," says Mladjenovic. "Static pricing means, 'here is my price, buy it or don't buy it, have a nice day.' Dynamic pricing is the whole point of an auction. As bidders, potential customers set the sale price starting with whatever minimum bid you stipulate."

don't want to put into the business don't stand liable for the business's debt. However, to take advantage of the protection a corporation offers, you must respect the corporation's identity. That means maintaining the corporation as a separate entity; keeping your corporate and personal funds separate, even if you are the sole shareholder; and following your state's rules regarding the holding of annual meetings and other record-keeping requirements. Do not expect a corporation to protect you personally against general liability issues, such as if someone is injured on your property or suffers an injury or damages due to your product or some other aspect of a business transaction with you. These days, lawyers sue both the corporation and the people involved, so protect yourself in that area with adequate insurance.

Is any one of these business structures better than another? No. We found eBay sellers operating as sole proprietors, partners, and corporations, and they made their choices based on what was best for their particular situation. For example, the reason Jonathan Garriss and his partner, David Topkins, chose to incorporate when they formed Gotham City Online was "planning for the future." The sole proprietors told us they simply didn't see a need to incorporate. Consider what you want to do now and where you expect to take your company, and then choose the form that is most appropriate for your particular needs.

If you decide to incorporate, do you need an attorney to set up the corporation? Again, no. There are plenty of good do-it-yourself books and kits on the market, and most of the state agencies that oversee corporations have guidelines you can use. Even so, it's always a good idea to have a lawyer at least look over your documents before you file them, just to make sure they are complete and will allow you to truly function as you want.

Beware!

Find out what types of licenses and permits are required for your business while you're still in the planning stage. You may find out that you can't legally operate the business you're envisioning, so give yourself time to make adjustments to your strategy before you've spent a lot of time and money trying to move in an impossible direction.

Finally, remember that your choice of legal structure is not an irrevocable decision, although if you're going to make a switch, it's easier to go from the simpler forms to the more sophisticated ones than the other way around. The typical pattern is to start as a sole proprietor and move up to a corporation as the business grows. But if you need the asset protection of a corporation from the beginning, start out that way.

Licenses and Permits

Most cities and counties require business operators to obtain various licenses and permits to comply with local regulations. While you're still in the planning stages, check with your local planning and zoning department or city/county business license department to find out what licenses and permits you will need and what is involved in obtaining them. You may need some or all of the following:

- *Occupational license or permit.* This is typically required by the city (or county if you are not within an incorporated city) for just about every business operating within its jurisdiction. License fees are essentially a tax, and the rates vary widely, based on the location and type of business. As part of the application process, the licensing bureau will check to make sure there are no zoning restrictions prohibiting you from operating in your location.

- *Fire department permit.* If your business is open to the public or in a commercial location (say your retail store has an eBay sales division, which you run onsite), you may be required to have a permit from the local fire department.

- *Sign permit.* Many cities and suburbs have sign ordinances that restrict the size, location, and sometimes the lighting and type of sign you can use in front of your business. Landlords may also impose their own restrictions. Most residential areas forbid signs altogether. To avoid costly mistakes, check regulations and secure the written approval of your landlord before you invest in a sign.

- *State licenses.* Many states require persons engaged in certain occupations to hold licenses or occupational permits. Often, these people must pass state examinations before they can conduct business. States commonly require licensing for auto mechanics, plumbers, electricians, building contractors, collection agents, insurance agents, real estate brokers, repossessors, and personal service providers such as doctors, nurses, barbers, cosmetologists, etc. It's unlikely that you will need a state license to sell your merchandise on eBay, but it's a good idea to check with your state's occupation licensing entity to be sure.

Business Insurance

It takes a lot to start a business, even a small one, so protect your investment with adequate insurance. If you're homebased, don't assume your homeowner's or renter's policy covers your business equipment; chances are, it doesn't. If you're located in a

> **Tip...**
>
> **Smart Tip**
> When you purchase insurance on your equipment and inventory, ask what documentation the insurance company requires before you ever have to file a claim. That way, you'll be sure to maintain appropriate records, and the claims process will be easier if it is ever necessary.

commercial facility, be prepared for your landlord to require proof of certain levels of liability insurance when you sign the lease. And in either case, you need coverage for your inventory and other valuables.

A smart approach to insurance is to find an agent who works with businesses similar to yours. The agent should be willing to help you analyze your needs, evaluate what risks you're willing to accept and what risks you need to insure against, and work with you to keep your insurance costs down.

Typically, homebased business owners should make sure their equipment and inventory are covered against theft, fire, flood, and other perils, and that they have some liability protection if someone (either a customer or an employee) is injured on their property or by their product. In most cases, one of the new insurance policies designed for homebased businesses will provide sufficient coverage. Also, if you use your vehicle for business, be sure it is appropriately covered.

If you opt for a commercial location, you'll find your landlord will probably require certain levels of general liability coverage as part of the terms of your lease. You'll also want to cover your inventory, equipment, and fixtures.

Once your business is up and running, consider purchasing business interruption insurance to replace lost revenue and cover related costs if you are ever unable to operate due to covered circumstances.

Depending on what you sell, you may need product liability insurance to protect you or your company financially if anything goes wrong with one of your products. It makes sense that the primary issue of product liability would fall back on the manufacturer, but in today's litigious society, everybody involved in the sale of the merchandise is likely to be named in a lawsuit. Sit down with your attorney and insurance agent to analyze your potential risks and exposures, and then purchase appropriate and adequate coverage.

In addition to property, casualty, and general liability, you may want to consider purchasing extra coverage that will pay if a claim against your basic policies exceeds their limits. This is known as an umbrella policy. Garriss says he has this type of coverage to protect his company in the event of a major catastrophe. Bob Willey of Trappe, Maryland's Bob's Neat Stuff also has an umbrella policy as added insurance for the items he sells on consignment. "I want to protect my clients' inventory," he says. "I also keep papers for the consignment listings in a separate area as proof of what I have on hand at any given time."

Professional Advisors

As a business owner, you may be the boss, but you can't be expected to know everything. You'll occasionally need to turn to professionals for information and assistance. It's a good idea to establish relationships with these professionals before you get into a crisis situation.

Smart Tip

Sit down with your insurance agent on an annual basis and review your insurance needs. As your company grows, it's sure to change. Also, insurance companies are always developing new products to meet the needs of the growing small-business market, and it's possible that one of these new policies will be appropriate for you.

To shop for a professional service provider, ask friends and associates for recommendations. You might also check with your local chamber of commerce or trade association for referrals. And don't overlook the Elance section of eBay.

Find someone who understands your industry and specific business, and who appears eager to work with you. Check them out with the Better Business Bureau and the appropriate state licensing agency before committing yourself to hiring them.

As an eBay seller, the professional service providers you're likely to need include:

- *Attorney*. You need a lawyer who practices in the area of business law, is honest, and appreciates your patronage. In most parts of the United States, there are many lawyers willing to compete fiercely for the privilege of serving you. Interview several, and choose one you feel comfortable with. Be sure to clarify the attorney's fee schedule ahead of time, and get your agreement in writing. Keep in mind that good commercial lawyers don't come cheap; if you want quality advice, you must be willing to pay for it. Your attorney should review all contracts, leases, letters of intent, and other legal documents before you sign them. He or she can also help you collect bad debts and establish personnel policies and procedures. Of course, if you are unsure of the legal ramifications of any situation, call your attorney immediately. In addition to using outside counsel, Andrew Robinson, co-owner of Boston Tables in Columbus, Ohio, says that his partner, Charles Kidder, is also an attorney—something that has been very helpful in business dealings.

- *Accountant*. Among your outside advisors, your accountant is likely to have the greatest impact on the success or failure of your business. If you are forming a corporation, your accountant should counsel you on tax issues during start-up. On an ongoing basis, your accountant can help you organize the statistical data concerning your business, assist in charting future actions based on

Staying Healthy with eBay

One of the biggest challenges of being self-employed or a small-business owner is finding affordable health insurance. As a service to eBay users who have achieved PowerSeller status, eBay has negotiated an agreement with a major insurance broker to provide a number of health insurance products, including major medical, dental, and pharmaceutical coverage. eBay does not subsidize the cost but rather has used the size of its user base in negotiating competitive rates for its members. However, it's a good idea to compare the programs available through eBay with other options you may have before making a decision.

▲

past performance, and advise you on your overall financial strategy regarding purchasing, capital investment, and other matters related to your business goals. A good accountant will also serve as a tax advisor, making sure you are in compliance with all applicable regulations and that you don't overpay any taxes.

- *Insurance agent.* A good independent insurance agent can assist you with all aspects of your business insurance, from general liability to employee benefits, and probably even handle your personal needs, as well. Look for an agent who works with a wide range of insurers and understands your particular business. This agent should be willing to explain the details of various types of coverage, consult with you to determine the most appropriate coverage, help you understand the degree of risk you are taking, work with you in developing risk-reduction programs, and assist in expediting any claims. "Our insurance agent has been fantastic in guiding us through this process," says Garriss. "Insurance is complex, and our insurance agent is one of the professionals we have depended on for good advice on something we had no idea about."

- *Banker.* You need a business bank account and a relationship with a banker. Don't just choose the bank you've always done your personal banking with; it may not be the best bank for your business. Interview several bankers before making a decision on where to place your business. Once your account is open, maintain a relationship with the banker. Periodically sit down and review your accounts and the services you use to make sure you are getting the package most appropriate for your situation. Ask for advice if you have financial questions or problems. When you need a loan or a bank reference to provide to creditors, the relationship you've established will work in your favor.

- *Consultants.* The consulting industry is booming, and for good reason. Consultants can provide valuable, objective input on all aspects of your business. Consider hiring a business consultant to evaluate your business plan or a marketing consultant to assist you in that area. When you are ready to hire employees, a human resources consultant may help you avoid some costly mistakes. Consulting fees vary widely, depending on the individual's experience, location, and field of expertise. If you can't afford to hire a consultant, consider hiring an MBA student from the business school at the nearest college or university.

- *Computer expert.* A computer is essential for doing business through online auctions and stores. In addition, you'll use your computer to manage your operation. Your computer and data are extremely valuable assets, so if you don't know much about computers, find someone to help you select a system and the appropriate software and to be available to help you maintain, troubleshoot, and expand your system as needed. If you're going to have a web site, consider hiring a professional to help you design it. Robinson says their company hired a college student as an intern to handle their computer needs and auction listings for the eBay side of the business.

Most of the eBay sellers we talked with have ongoing relationships with accountants and know of an attorney they can call on if they need one. Many use computer consultants to assist with custom software development and web designers to create a professional online image. Let professionals help you with the activities that are essential to the profitable functioning of your business but are not the core of your operation. That will free you up to focus on building and growing your company.

Start-Up Economics and Financial Management

There are two key sides to the issue of money: how much you need to start and operate, and how much you can expect to make. Analyzing these numbers is often extremely difficult for small-business owners who would rather be in the trenches getting the work done than bound to a desk dealing with tiresome numbers. Because most eBay sellers get started with equipment and inventory they already own, it's easy to overlook the process of creating a sound financial plan. And if you're treating your eBay sales as a hobby that happens to generate a little extra money, it's OK if you don't do much planning. But if you want to create a real business, you need to be prepared to deal with start-up economics and ongoing financial management.

Where Will You Find Start-Up Money?

As you're putting together your financial plan, consider these sources of start-up funds:

- *Your own resources.* Do a thorough inventory of your assets. People generally have more assets than they immediately realize. This could include savings accounts, equity in real estate, retirement accounts, vehicles, recreation equipment, collections, and other investments. You may opt to sell assets for cash, or use them as collateral for a loan. Many eBay sellers auction things they already own to raise the cash they need to invest in more inventory. For example, part-time sellers Gary and Susan Marler of Selma, North Carolina, generated about $1,000 selling miscellaneous items from around their house, and used that money to invest in more inventory. Take a look, too, at your personal line of credit; most of the equipment you'll need is available through retail stores, web sites, and eBay sellers that accept credit cards.

- *Friends and family.* The logical next step after tapping your own resources is to approach friends and relatives who believe in you and want to help you succeed. Be cautious with these arrangements, though; no matter how close you are, present yourself professionally, put everything in writing, and be sure the individuals you approach can afford to take the risk of investing in your business.

- *Partners.* Although most operations that sell on eBay are owned by just one person, you may want to consider using the "strength in numbers" principle and look for someone who may want to team up with you in your venture. You may choose someone who has financial resources and wants to work side by side with you in the business. Or you may find someone who has money to invest but no interest in doing the actual work. Be sure to create a written partnership agreement that clearly defines your respective responsibilities and obligations.

- *Government programs.* Take advantage of the abundance of local, state, and federal programs designed to support small businesses. Make your first stop the SBA; then investigate various other programs. Women, minorities, and veterans should check out niche financing possibilities designed to help these groups get into business. The business section of your local library is a good place to begin your research.

How Much Do You Need?

It takes very little cash to just sell things on eBay, especially if you already have a business. However, if you purchase stock, and certainly as you grow, you'll need money to invest in inventory, facilities, and more sophisticated equipment. The eBay sellers we talked with started on eBay with very little capital and used the revenue they generated to grow their operations.

Jonathan Garriss says it took about $600 to get Gotham City Online started—that was the cost of the computer and camera he and his partner purchased on eBay. David Lynn, CRI's IT director, spent nothing. He was already running a wholesale manufacturing business when his company began selling on eBay, so he already had the necessary computer equipment and inventory.

Tustin, California, eBay seller Linda Parker started with a computer and a digital camera—she already owned the computer, and the camera was a Valentine's Day gift from her husband. "Not very romantic, but very practical," she says. Along those lines, Oviedo, Florida, eBay entrepreneur Liz Baker was happy to get a set of postal scales as her Mother's Day present one year.

The Marlers' start-up costs for their part-time eBay selling operation were zero. "We needed a computer, a scanner and a camera—all of which we already owned, so there were no start-up costs," Susan says.

Calculate how much you need to start your ideal business, and then figure out how much you have. If you have all the cash you need, you're fortunate. If you don't, you need to start playing with the numbers and deciding what you can do without.

> **Smart Tip**
> *Tip...*
> Christmas items will sell year-round, but you'll get the best prices in October, November and December.

The chart starting on page 98 gives you a list of the start-up equipment you're likely to need and the approximate cost of each item. Use it as a guide to put together your start-up budget.

Pricing

In a traditional retail situation, you would buy your stock, mark it up according to a formula you felt was fair and reasonable, and put it out for sale. In an auction, the buyer determines the final selling price. Even so, you need to understand pricing so you can set your minimum bids and reserve amounts if you use them, as well as price the items in your eBay store.

Start-Up Expenses

Item	Price
Computer and Office Equipment and Supplies	
Computer system (with printer)	$1,500–4,500
Digital camera	$130–500
Scanner	$100–600
Fax machine	$100–250
Multifunction device (fax/copier/printer/scanner)	$200–900
Two-line full-featured phone system	$40–150
Voice mail	$6–20/month
E-mail	$0–25/month
Web site design	$500–5,000
Web site hosting	$20–200/month
Uninterruptible power supply	$125–250
Zip drive backup	$100–300
Surge protector	$15–60
Calculator	$5–50
Copier	$100–1,000+
Desk	$50–250
Desk chair	$50–200
Printer stand	$50–75
File cabinet(s)	$40–100
Bookcase	$70–100
Computer/copier paper	$25–50/case

Start-Up Expenses, continued

Item	Price
Business cards	$6–12
Letterhead paper and envelopes	$50–125
Address stamp	$10
Extra printer cartridge	$25–80
Extra fax cartridge	$30–90
Zip drive disks	$10–45
Mouse pad	$3–20
Miscellaneous office supplies	$100–150
Storage shelves, cabinets	$100–500
Shipping Equipment and Supplies	
Hand truck	$30–209
High-speed tape dispenser	$18–30
Carton stapler	$200–500
Electronic scale	$50–715
Paper shredder	$25–180
Sealing tape	$5–8
Boxes	$225–400
Bubble wrap (100-foot roll)	$10–20/roll
Mailing labels	$75–200
Cushioned mailers	$150–250
Packing materials	$50–350

An aspect to pricing that is critical to profitable eBay selling is understanding value, says consultant Paul Mladjenovic. If you just want to clear out your garage, value is not as important as it is if you want to build a profitable business selling on eBay. But even in that case, you want to get the best price possible, and understanding value will help you do that.

A key element to consider when pricing is what similar items have sold for. You can search eBay for completed auctions and study the bid patterns and winning bids. Parker researches what similar items have sold for and sets her minimum bids lower than that figure.

In fact, many eBay sellers set their opening bid low—often as low as a dollar—and trust the market to drive up the price to a profitable level. That works for Baker, who often starts the bidding for her auctions at $1 and seldom uses a reserve. "eBay is a unique marketplace," Baker notes. "When you put something up for $1 with no reserve, it can sell for more than if you put it up with a $100 reserve. Once a bid is placed, people become emotionally attached to the item and find it hard to let go, which is why many bidding wars break out at the last minute."

In Granville, Michigan, eBay seller Laurie Ayers often uses the amount she paid for an item as her starting point. "I don't like to start anything below $1.99 or $2," she says. But her experience has been that setting the starting bid lower means a higher final bid price. She believes a higher starting bid may scare off bidders looking for a bargain, but a lower starting figure can generate enough interest to start a bidding war.

PowerSeller Bob Willey in Trappe, Maryland, feels that when you have unique items that are sought after, the starting price really doesn't matter much. He thinks if people want it they are going to pay whatever they need to get it, and that often helps to build the "auction frenzy."

Andrew Robinson of Boston Tables in Columbus, Ohio, says he uses different strategies when setting prices. "A lot of it depends on what our competition is doing, as well as what is going on in the market," he says. "If another seller is starting a similar item at a very low price, we will try to compete with that in the auction environment." Robinson feels that auction listings are more of a marketing tool to draw shoppers into their eBay store. If they do take a hit and sell a pool table at a loss, the store profits are more than sufficient to absorb those losses.

Susan Marler considers the cost of the item as well as the market when pricing. "I start by looking through current and completed auctions to see what the lowest and highest bids were, and then I'll typically start somewhere in the middle," she says. "If it's something that I have personally owned and is not of value to me, I generally start the bidding around 99 cents to bring in lookers. But if it's something that I purchased elsewhere—new or used—I will start the auction a few dollars over my cost." Marler figures that most eBay shoppers are bargain hunters like herself and doesn't mind offering great deals, as long as she can make a profit.

When pricing items for Gotham City Online, Garriss uses a different strategy: He considers his cost and what he thinks the merchandise will sell for. "We are not in the camp of starting things at a dollar and let's see what happens," he says.

How much profit should you make? There's no hard and fast rule or a clear definition of how much profit means you are successful. In general, however, when buying items at wholesale to sell retail, look for a gross profit of at least 15 percent.

Will you ever sell an item for less than it cost you? Probably. Will you sell an item for more than you thought it was worth? Again, probably. Just know that with experience, your pricing skills will sharpen.

Taxing Matters

A potentially sticky area for online auction sellers is sales tax. Many large retailers with online operations have begun collecting sales tax on their internet sales, and legislation affecting how internet sales are taxed is pending at state and federal levels. As a business owner, you are responsible for knowing the law and doing the right thing. In Plano, Texas, clothing seller Georgene Harkness says that when an auction closes, she prints out an invoice for her records from My eBay and hand-marks the top of the page with "State" if the item was sold to someone in her state. "I never throw away invoices," she says. "A sales tax auditor is going to want to see all of them, not just the in-state ones."

Whether or not you need to collect and remit state and local sales tax depends on a variety of factors, including your product line, where your business is located, and where your customers are. Also, many states have what's known as casual sale exemptions that might apply if you're just selling your own items in what amounts to an online garage sale.

"You need to know the rules of the state you're in," advises Chuck Norman, CPA, a partner with Ernst & Young in Toledo, Ohio. "Talk to your accountant or contact your state's revenue service, and be sure you clearly understand the rules as they apply to your business."

To charge and collect sales tax, you'll need a sales tax ID number (sometimes referred to as a reseller's permit). This is usually a very simple process; just check with your state's department of revenue for information on how to proceed.

▲

How Will You Get Paid?

Most internet shoppers want instant gratification. They want to buy something online, win an auction, pay quickly and easily, and have their merchandise on their doorstep as soon as possible. Most don't want to mail you a check and wait for it to arrive, get deposited, and clear the bank before you ship their goods. And they're probably not thrilled about going to the hassle of buying a money order or getting a certified check. So if you're going to sell online, you should take some type of credit card, either with your own merchant account or with eBay's popular PayPal service.

PayPal is an eBay company that allows you to accept credit card, bank account, and PayPal account balance payments over the internet. While there are other payment services (see the "Payment Resources" section in this book's Appendix for a list), PayPal provides a fast, easy, secure way for people to exchange funds online.

PayPal is accepted in over 90 percent of eBay listings in the United States, and three out of four eBay buyers prefer to pay with PayPal. One reason for its popularity is that PayPal offers a Seller Protection Policy that protects sellers against chargebacks. (PayPal also offers a PayPal Buyer Protection Program, which covers buyers up to $1,000 on a transaction.)

PayPal has a limit of $10,000 per transaction. There is no charge to open a PayPal account or to make payments using PayPal. Buyers can fund a PayPal payment using their PayPal account balance, checking account, or credit cards.

As a seller, you must have a Premier or Business account so that you can accept credit card as well as bank payments (sellers are charged a small fee to receive funds).

> ## ⚠ Beware!
> Mail thieves operate even in the nicest of neighborhoods. To keep checks and money orders secure, open a private mailbox at the post office or mail center to use for business instead of using your home address.

PayPal charges two fees: the standard rate, which is 2.9 percent plus 30 cents per transaction, and the merchant rate, which is between 1.9 percent and 2.5 percent plus 30 cents per transaction. The qualification for the merchant rate is $3,000 per month in payment volume.

Some of PayPal's Premier Account benefits include the ability to receive any type of payment, including credit cards, for low fees; access to an exclusive customer service hotline; and use of special sellers tools. With a Business Account, you can use all the features of a Premier Account, have multiple logins, and do business under a corporate name.

PayPal offers a variety of auction tools that sellers can use to help automate their listings. For instance, when new auctions are launched, the PayPal logo will be inserted so that buyers will know you accept this form of payment. End-of-auction e-mails that send the buyer shipping and payment instructions can be automatically generated. You have the ability to access sales reports to help manage closing transactions more efficiently. Perhaps one of the best features of using PayPal in your auctions is the Shipping Center because you can calculate and pay for shipping and insurance through your account. Liz Baker loves this feature because she can quickly print out a mailing label that includes the correct postage and have the funds simultaneously withdrawn from her PayPal account. She says, "It just doesn't get any easier than that."

Escrow Services

For higher-priced items, many buyers like to use an escrow service, which means that the winning bidder sends the payment to a neutral third party (an escrow company) to be held until the goods are shipped and the bidder is satisfied with their condition.

The benefit of escrow is that the escrow company is neutral, so both the buyer and seller are protected. Of course, you'll pay for this service; the fee varies depending on the details of the transaction.

With escrow, the buyer is protected because the seller isn't paid until the merchandise is delivered and inspected. The seller is protected because he doesn't ship the goods until the escrow service verifies receipt of the funds.

Be sure the escrow company you choose is legitimate and licensed. Don't be offended if buyers want to check out the escrow company before sending money— and when you're buying, you should do the same.

Credit Card Fraud

Credit card fraud is a significant problem for buyers, sellers, and credit card issuers. For card-present, in-store transactions, liability for fraud belongs to the credit card issuer. For card-not-present transactions, including online transactions, liability for fraud shifts to the seller. That means sellers don't receive payment for fraudulent online transactions. Don't let this stop you from doing business online, but take steps to limit your risk.

Dollar Stretcher

If you start your business using equipment you already own, you may be able to deduct a portion of the cost of that equipment as a business expense on your tax return. Check with your tax advisor for guidance.

One of your most important fraud prevention steps is to deal with established, reputable merchant account providers (the acquiring bank) and processors. Your payment gateway provider (where authorizations and payments are processed) should offer real-time credit card authorization results to prevent charges on cards that have been reported as lost or stolen, or that are no longer valid for any other reason.

Use an address verification service that matches the cardholder billing address on file with the billing address submitted. Use card security codes, which are numbers that appear on Visa, MasterCard, and American Express cards that are never printed on receipts. The ability of a customer to provide these codes is additional assurance that the actual card is in the possession of the person conducting the transaction.

Monitor your transactions for suspicious activity. Watch for multiple orders purchased on the same credit card for items such as electronics, which are easily resold. Finally, develop a negative card and shipping address list and crosscheck orders against it. Many criminals will return to the same merchant to make fraudulent transactions.

Keeping Records

There are many reasons why you need to keep good records on your income and expenses, including the fact that you need to know whether or not you are making a profit, what particular items are more profitable than others, and how much you have to pay in taxes. Before you launch your business, set up a system that allows you to keep complete and detailed records on everything you spend and earn.

Tax Attack

Businesses are required to pay a wide range of taxes, and there are no exceptions for companies that sell on eBay. Keep good records so you can offset your local, state, and federal income taxes with your operating expenses. If you have employees, you'll be responsible for payroll taxes. If you operate as a corporation, you'll have to pay payroll taxes for yourself; as a sole proprietor, you'll pay self-employment tax. Then there are property taxes, taxes on your equipment and inventory, fees and taxes to maintain your corporate status, your business license fee (which is really a tax), and other lesser-known taxes.

Chuck Norman, CPA, a partner with Ernst & Young in Toledo, Ohio, advises sitting down with a competent tax advisor to be sure you understand all your responsibilities and obligations regarding local, state, and federal taxes. You also want to be sure to take every deduction to which you are entitled, and report all your income. Failing to report income on your tax return is a crime and can land you in a lot of trouble. If you have employees, you need to understand and follow the rules regarding payroll taxes. Your tax advisor can guide you on any other applicable tax issues.

You can keep your records manually or use any of the popular off-the-shelf accounting systems available today. Choose the system that's easiest for you.

Monitoring Your Financial Progress

One of the key indicators of the overall health of your business is its financial status, and it's important to monitor your financial progress closely. The only way you can do that is to keep good records. An alternative is to ask your accountant for assistance in setting up your system. The key is to do it correctly and completely from the very beginning, and keep your records current and accurate throughout the life of your company.

Keeping good records helps generate the financial statements that tell you exactly where you stand and what you need to do next. The key financial statements you need to understand and use regularly are:

- *Profit and loss statement (also called the P&L or the income statement).* This statement illustrates how much your company is making or losing over a designated period—monthly, quarterly, or annually—by subtracting expenses from your revenue to arrive at a net result, which is either a profit or a loss.

- *Balance sheet.* A balance sheet is a table showing your assets, liabilities, and capital at a specific point; a balance sheet is typically generated monthly, quarterly, or annually when the books are closed.

- *Cash flow statement.* This summarizes the operating, investing, and financing activities of your business as they relate to the inflow and outflow of cash; as with the profit and loss statement, a cash flow statement is prepared to reflect a specific accounting period, such as monthly, quarterly, or annually.

Successful eBay sellers review these reports regularly, at least monthly, so they always know where they stand and can quickly move to correct minor difficulties before they become major financial problems.

Locating and
Setting Up Your
Business

The flexibility of selling on eBay gives you a lot of choices in where to locate your operation and how to get it set up. You can opt for a retail store or a warehouse location, or you can work from home.

▲

Because of the room required to store inventory and handle shipping, homebased eBay sellers will find their growth limited by the space they have available. Whether or not this is a problem for you depends on your own personal goals. If you are looking to create a sizable company with several employees and generate hundreds of thousands of dollars each year in sales, there's no question about it—you'll need a commercial location. But if your goal is a small business that generates a comfortable income for you, being homebased may be the ideal situation. A variety of other business goals and situations fall between those two extremes, so think about what your goals are, and then consider your various location options.

The Home Advantage

The decision to set up your business at home will depend on a number of things, including local zoning codes, your landlord (if you have one), your family situation, your budget, and your own plans for how you want to operate your company.

A particular challenge to operating a homebased eBay business is that it can take up a lot of room. You'll need a place to set up your desk and computer, an area for staging product photographs, an area for packing and shipping tasks, and storage for your inventory and supplies.

Ideally, you should have a section of your home you can set aside for exclusive business use, but that's not always practical or possible. Tustin, California, eBay seller Linda Parker has her desk and computer in one room, with her inventory stored on a high shelf that runs the perimeter of her kitchen—"that keeps breakables away from my little one's hands," she says—and her packing and shipping area in the garage.

Part-time seller Liz Baker's eBay operation in Oviedo, Florida, is more physically focused. "I have an office with lots of bookshelves, plus a closet in that room filled with eBay things," she says. Trading Assistant Bob Willey has his eBay operation in Trappe, Maryland, set up in a 700-square-foot area that is isolated from the rest of the house and includes a separate entrance for customers.

The most obvious advantage of being homebased, especially in the beginning, is the small initial capital outlay. The money you might otherwise have spent on leasing commercial space can be invested in your inventory or on marketing and promotional expenses.

A homebased business also offers substantial tax breaks, but you must be sure your setup meets IRS requirements. According to *The Ernst & Young Tax Guide* (John Wiley & Sons), the IRS says that certain expenses are deductible if part of your home is "your principal place of business for any trade or business in which you engage, or [it is] a place to meet or deal with your patients, clients or customers in the normal course of your trade or business." But you must choose a room—and to take the home office deduction it must not be just a corner of a room—to use solely as your office and/or workroom. If it also contains a TV or stereo and serves as a den or guest room, or if you work on the dining room table, your home office deduction probably will not hold up under an IRS audit. For example, Parker's setup likely wouldn't qualify, but Willey's and Baker's would.

What can you deduct? Directly related expenses, which are those that benefit only the business part of your home, and a portion of indirect expenses, which are the costs involved in keeping up and running your entire home. For example, your office furniture and equipment are fully deductible as directly related expenses. In the area of indirect expenses, you may deduct a portion of your household utilities and services (electric, gas, water, sewage, trash collection, etc.) based on the percentage of space you use for business purposes. Other examples of indirect expenses include real estate taxes, deductible mortgage interest, casualty losses, rent, insurance, repairs, security systems, and depreciation.

Before you invest too much time in planning or setting up a homebased operation, check your local zoning codes and any deed restrictions that may be attached to the property. Many municipalities have ordinances that limit the nature and volume of commercial activities that can occur in residential areas. Some outright prohibit the establishment of homebased businesses. Others may allow such enterprises but place restrictions regarding issues such as signage, traffic, employees, commercially marked vehicles, and noise. Find out what, if any, ordinances are in place regarding homebased businesses before applying for your business license; you may need to adjust your plan to be in compliance. Call your city hall's general information number and ask to be referred to the appropriate department—usually the planning and zoning department, or perhaps the business and occupational licensing office. Don't ask the clerk for advice; instead, get a copy of any ordinances concerning homebased businesses and the specific zoning code that applies to your property. You may need to consult an attorney who can interpret the fine points of the ordinance. Also, there is often a substantial difference between what an ordinance says and the way it is enforced.

If your business will violate the zoning code, you may still be able to operate by applying for a variance or conditional-use permit. Or you can apply to have the zoning changed. Both these processes are lengthy and require a significant amount of documentation, so you should seriously consider everything involved before you begin the process.

> **Dollar Stretcher**
>
> Even if your homebased office setup does not meet IRS requirements that would allow you to deduct those expenses, you can still deduct other expenses—inventory, storage, equipment, shipping, automobile, marketing, etc.—that are legitimate costs of doing business.

▲

Going Retail

You have a number of options if you decide to open a retail store, and what you choose depends on the products you're selling. Understand that the face-to-face retail side of your operation will be very different from your eBay side. With that in mind, some of the factors you need to consider when deciding on a retail location for your business are:

- *Anticipated sales volume.* How will the location contribute to your sales volume? Consider the presence or potential presence of other businesses that will compete with you, and be sure the market is strong enough to support all of you.

- *Accessibility to potential customers.* Consider how easy it will be for customers to get to your business. If vehicle traffic on the street where you'll be located is often heavy, or if the speed limit is more than 35 mph, drivers may have difficulty entering or leaving your site. Narrow entrances and exits, turns that are hard to negotiate, and parking lots that are always full are deterrents that can prevent would-be customers from patronizing your shop. If you are relying on strong pedestrian traffic, consider whether or not nearby businesses will generate foot traffic for you. Large department stores will draw many customers, and shopping centers in busy office districts might attract pedestrian shoppers, particularly during weekday lunch hours. By contrast, a strip center anchored by a supermarket may not be the best location; grocery shoppers rarely browse through a strip mall either before or after they do their food buying. Consider the entrance to the site. Is it on the street level or an upper floor? Can it be reached from a main street, or is it difficult to find? Take some time to analyze the site. Monitor foot and auto traffic patterns at different times of the day. See if those patterns fit the hours you want to do business. Visit the prospective site on several different days to assess any changes in the pattern.

- *Rent-paying capacity of your business.* The best locations will usually command the highest rents. If you've done a sales and profit projection for your first year of operation, you will know approximately how much revenue you can expect to generate, and you can use that information to decide how much rent you can afford to pay.

- *Restrictive ordinances.* You may encounter unusually restrictive ordinances that make an otherwise strong site less than ideal, such as limitations on the hours of the day when trucks can legally load or unload. Cities and towns are composed of areas—from a few blocks to many acres in size—zoned only for commercial, industrial, or residential development. Each zone may have its own restrictions. A commercial zone may permit one type of business but not another, so check the zoning codes of any potential location before pursuing a specific site or spending a lot of time and money on a market survey.

- *Traffic density.* Modern site analysis distinguishes between automobile and pedestrian traffic. If auto traffic were the only type of traffic important to a profitable operation, most businesses would be located near highways or main roads. Given that so many successful businesses are located on side streets away from busy roads, you clearly need to consider pedestrian traffic as well. With careful examination of foot traffic, you can determine the approximate sales potential of each pedestrian passing a given location. Two factors are especially important in this analysis: total pedestrian traffic during business hours and the percentage of that traffic that's likely to enter your shop.

- *Customer parking facilities.* The site should provide convenient and adequate parking, as well as easy access for customers. Storefront parking is always better than a rear lot; people like to be able to see the parking lot before they turn off the main thoroughfare. The lot should be well-lit and secure. Consider whether the parking area will need expansion, resurfacing, or striping—possibly at an additional cost to you. If you're looking at a free-standing location, think big and envision how you will accommodate the customers your business will eventually attract.

- *Proximity to other businesses.* Neighboring businesses may influence your store's volume, and their presence can work for you or against you. Studies of the natural clustering of businesses show that certain types of companies do well when located close to one another. For example, men's and women's apparel and variety stores are commonly located near department stores. Restaurants, barbershops, and candy, tobacco, and jewelry stores are often found near theaters. Florists are often grouped with shoe stores and women's clothing stores.

- *History of the site.* Find out the recent history of each site under consideration before you make a final selection. Who were the previous tenants, and why are they no longer there? There are sites—in malls and shopping centers, as well

Combo Deal

Choosing your location doesn't have to mean deciding between home and an office. If you like working at home but still need retail space or commercial storage, simply operate from more than one location. Consider renting one or two warehouses where products are received, stored, and packaged for shipping, and do the administrative work at your home office.

as in free-standing locations—that have been occupied by successions of business failures. The reasons for the failures may be completely unrelated to the success potential of your operation, or they could mean your business will meet the same fate. You need to study and understand why previous tenants failed so you can avoid repeating their mistakes.

> **Bright Idea**
>
> Hang wall clocks set to different time zones in your office. You'll be able to see at a glance what time it is where your customers are, rather than having to do the calculation in your head before you place a call or leave a message.

- *Terms of the lease.* Be sure you understand all the details of the lease because it's possible that an excellent site may have unacceptable leasing terms. The time to negotiate terms is before you sign the lease; don't wait until you've moved in to try to change the terms.

- *Rent-advertising relationship.* You may need to account for up to six months of advertising and promotion expenditures in your working capital. Few businesses can succeed without any sales promotion, and the larger the sum you can afford for well-placed, well-targeted advertising and promotions, the greater your chances of success. The amount you plan to spend on advertising may be closely related to your site choice and the proposed rent. If you locate in a shopping center or mall supported by huge ad budgets and the presence of large, popular chain and department stores, you will most likely generate revenue from the first day you open your doors—with no individual advertising at all. Of course, your rent will be proportionately higher than that of an independent location. If you don't locate in an area that attracts a lot of foot traffic, you will experience a slower growth rate, even if your business fronts a high-traffic street. Your real profits will come as you develop a customer base—and this will require advertising and promotion. Both center developers and tenants recommend that operators just starting out begin in small community centers and then graduate to larger regional centers or malls.

Nonretail Commercial

If you don't want to—or simply don't have the room to—operate from home, but you don't want to build a retail business, consider leasing space in a warehouse or light industrial facility.

If your inventory includes temperature-sensitive items, be sure the facility is adequately air conditioned. Also, thoroughly research security and accessibility issues, especially if you expect to be working late at night or on weekends.

When Andrew Robinson started Boston Tables, he and his wife ran the business from their home and stored the products in a public fulfillment warehouse. But that arrangement only lasted about six months as the company grew and needed more space. He now has a 15,000-square-foot warehouse, plus an additional warehouse they use as flex space during seasonal times.

Dollar Stretcher

When looking for stock to buy, watch for great deals from sellers who have lost their storage space or who don't have room to store everything they have. When circumstances force someone to sell quickly, the buyer usually benefits.

Equipping Your
eBay Business

Most eBay sellers start their businesses with equipment they already own, and you'll probably do the same. That's what makes selling on eBay such an attractive business proposition. Even though you can get started with just your computer and either a digital camera or scanner, there are lots of other pieces of equipment that range from helpful to

▲

essential, depending on your particular operation. You don't need every single piece of equipment listed in this chapter to get started, but you should consider each one and decide how it works in relation to your own goals and growth strategy.

Basic Office Equipment

Many entrepreneurs find a trip to the local office supply and equipment store more exciting than an excursion to any mall. It's easy to get carried away when you're surrounded with an abundance of clever gadgets, all designed to make your working life easier and more fun. But if, like most new business owners, you're starting on a budget, discipline yourself and buy only what you need. Consider these basic items:

- *Typewriter.* You may think that most typewriters are in museums these days, but they actually remain quite useful to businesses that deal frequently with preprinted and multipart forms, such as order forms and shipping documents. The determination of whether or not you need a typewriter is one only you can make based on your specific operation. A good electric typewriter can be purchased for $100 to $150.

- *Computer and printer.* A computer is absolutely essential if you're going to be selling on eBay. In addition, it can help you manage complex bookkeeping and inventory control tasks, maintain customer records, and produce marketing materials. You don't necessarily need the "latest and greatest" in computer power, but you need a system with the most current version of Windows, a 2.4GHz Pentium 4 processor or Athlon XP 2100+, 512MB to 1GB RAM, an 80GB or bigger hard drive, a CD-ROM drive (48X or better), a 56 Kbps modem, and a 32MB video card. You should expect to spend $1,500 to $2,000 for your computer and an additional $100 to $1,000 for a printer (color inkjets will run $100 to $500; laser printers range from $300 to $1,000).

- *Software.* Think of software as your computer's "brains"—the instructions that tell your computer how to accomplish the functions you need. There are many programs on the market that will handle your accounting, inventory, customer information management, and other administrative requirements. Software can be a significant investment, so do a careful analysis of your own needs, and then study the market and examine a variety of products before making a final decision.

- *Modem.* Modems are necessary to access online services and the internet and have become a standard component of most computers. Serious eBay sellers don't have time to wait for a telephone dial-up modem to upload photos or browse web pages at a leisurely pace; consider investing in a high-speed modem for quicker, more efficient operations. As an alternative to the modem that comes with a computer, you may want to purchase a cable modem (about $200 plus a monthly fee of about $40); a DSL terminal or modem ($200 to $500, plus a monthly fee of $30 to $40); or an ISDN terminal or modem (about $250 plus $50 per month).

- *Data and equipment protection.* You need an uninterruptible power supply to keep your computer from going down in the event of a power failure or brownout, as well as a surge protector to protect your system from power surges. You can buy these items separately or as a combined unit. You'll also need a data backup system that allows you to copy the information from your computer to another location for safe storage.

- *Photocopier.* The photocopier is a fixture of the modern office and can be very useful to even the smallest business. At the least, it will come in handy when you have to copy documentation in the event you have a damage claim with a shipping company. The larger your operation, the more likely you are to need to make photocopies of a variety of things. You can get a basic, low-end, no-frills personal copier for $100 to $500 in just about any office supply store. More elaborate models increase proportionately in price. If you anticipate a heavy copy volume, consider leasing a photocopier.

- *Fax machine.* Most eBay sellers communicate by e-mail or phone and rarely need to send documents by fax. As with a photocopier, the larger your operation, the greater the chance that you'll need fax capabilities. If or when you do, you can either add a fax card to your computer or buy a stand-alone machine. If you use your computer, it must be on to send or receive faxes, and the transmission may interrupt other work. For many businesses, a stand-alone machine on a dedicated telephone line is a wise investment. Expect to pay about $100 for a single-function plain-paper fax to $200 to $900 for a multifunction device (fax/copier/printer/scanner).

 Beware!
Though integrated, multifunction devices—such as a copier/printer/fax machine or a fax/telephone/answering machine—may cost less to acquire and take up less space in your office, you risk losing all these functions simultaneously if the equipment fails. Also, consider your anticipated volume of use with the machine's efficiency rating and cost to operate, and compare that to stand-alone machines before making a final decision.

- *Postage scale.* A postage scale is a valuable investment for eBay sellers. An accurate scale takes the guesswork out of postage and will quickly pay for itself. It's a good idea to weigh every piece of mail—both envelopes and packages—to eliminate the risk of items being returned for insufficient postage or overpaying if you are unsure of the weight. Mechanical scales typically range from $10 to $25 and will be sufficient as you are getting started. As your sales volume increases, you'll want a digital scale, which is somewhat more expensive—generally from $50 to $200—but significantly more accurate than a mechanical unit. Or you may want to invest in an electronic computing scale that weighs the item and then calculates the rate via the carrier of your choice, making it easy for you to make price and service comparisons. Programmable electronic scales range in price from $80 to $250.

- *Postage meter.* Postage meters allow you to pay for postage in advance and print the exact amount on the mailing piece when it is used. Meters also provide a professional image, are more convenient than stamps, and can save you money in a number of ways. Postage meters are leased, not sold, with rates starting at about $20 per month, or you can get a meter/electronic scale combo for $20 to $120 per month. They require a license, which is available from your local post office. Only four manufacturers are licensed by the U.S. Postal Service to manufacture and lease postage meters; your local post office can provide you with contact information. Smaller eBay sellers find that buying postage online is an affordable and convenient alternative to leasing a postage meter.

- *Paper shredder.* A response to both a growing concern for privacy and the need to recycle and conserve space in landfills, shredders are becoming increasingly common in both homes and offices. They allow you to efficiently destroy incoming unsolicited direct mail, as well as sensitive internal documents before they are discarded. Shredded paper can be compacted much tighter than paper tossed in a wastebasket, and it can also be used as packing material. Light-duty shredders start at about $25, and heavier-capacity shredders run from $80 to $180.

Telecommunications

The ability to communicate quickly with your customers, employees, and suppliers is essential to any business. Advancing technology gives you a wide range of telecommunications options. Most telephone companies have created departments dedicated to small and homebased businesses; contact your local telephone service provider and ask to speak with someone who can review your needs and help you put together a service and equipment package that will work for you. Specific elements to keep in mind include:

- *Telephone.* If you're homebased, a single voice telephone line should be adequate during the start-up period. As you grow and your call volume increases, you'll add more lines. However, if you're in a commercial location or if you plan on using the phone a lot if you're homebased, you should have two phone lines from the start.

    Your telephone can be a tremendous productivity tool, and most of the models on the market today are rich in features you will find useful. Such features include automatic redial, which redials the last number called at regular intervals until the call is completed; programmable memory for storing frequently called numbers; and speakerphone for hands-free use. You may also want call forwarding, which allows you to forward calls to another number when you're not at your desk, and call waiting, which signals you that another call is coming in while you are on the phone. These services are typically available through your telephone company for a monthly fee.

    If you are going to be spending a great deal of time on the phone, consider using a headset for comfort and efficiency. A cordless phone lets you move around freely while talking, but these units vary widely in price and quality, so research them thoroughly before making a purchase.

- *Answering machine/voice mail.* Because your business phone should never go unanswered, you need some sort of reliable answering device to take calls when you can't do it yourself. Whether you buy an answering machine (expect to pay $15 to $65 for a basic model or $100 to $200 for one with advanced features) or use the voice-mail service provided through your telephone company (anywhere from $6 to $20 per month) is a choice you must make depending on your personal preferences, work style, and needs.

- *Cell phone.* Once considered a luxury, cell phones are almost as common as landlines and have even replaced landlines for many users. Most have features similar to your office phone—such as caller ID, call waiting, and voice mail—and equipment and service packages are very reasonably priced. Features such as digital images, text messaging, e-mail, news services, and more are becoming increasingly available and affordable. Cell phones are especially convenient for eBay sellers who spend a lot of time shopping at garage sales, flea markets, and thrift shops for their inventory. You can even sign up to have free eBay alerts sent to your cell phone, which notify you when an auction ends or you have been outbid.

▲

- *Pager.* A pager lets you know that someone is trying to reach you and lets you decide when to return the call. Many people use pagers in conjunction with cell phones to conserve the cost of airtime. Ask prospective pager suppliers if your system can be set up so you are paged whenever someone leaves a message in your voice-mail box. This service allows you to retrieve your messages immediately and eliminates having to periodically check to see if anyone has called. As with cell phones, the pager industry is very competitive, so shop around for the best deal. Expect to pay about $72 per year.

- *Toll-free number.* You may want to consider providing your customers with a toll-free number so they can reach you without having to make a long-distance call. Most long-distance service providers offer toll-free numbers and have a wide range of service and price packages. Shop around to find the best deal for you.

- *E-mail.* E-mail allows for fast, efficient, 24-hour communication, and it's an essential tool for eBay sellers. Consider setting up a separate e-mail address for your eBay selling activities to help you manage your business correspondence more effectively. Check your messages regularly and reply to them promptly. E-mail costs range from free to $25 per month.

Other Equipment

In addition to these basics, there are other items you may need, depending on your particular operation. They include:

- *Digital camera.* Besides your computer, the most important piece of equipment for an eBay seller is a digital camera. Yes, you can use a traditional film camera, but that means you spend time and money on processing, and then you have to scan the picture before you can put up the auction. And if your pictures don't turn out well, you have to shoot them again and wait for them to be developed before launching your auction. Be sure to get a good-quality digital camera, one that will show the detail of your products. There are many digital cameras on the market, and new technologies are being introduced regularly. If you don't know much about digital cameras, use the discussion board feature in eBay's "Community" section to get input from other users about which camera brands and models work well and which ones don't.

Bright Idea

If you have employees, get their input when making purchasing decisions on supplies and equipment. The people who are using these items every day know best what works and what doesn't, what is efficient and what isn't.

- *Scanner.* Even if you have a digital camera, a scanner can be useful. Sometimes you'll have manufacturer's photos of a product that you can scan in and use, instead of—or in addition to—your own pictures. If you are selling two-dimensional items, such as trading cards and photographs, you can use a scanner to create the image that will accompany your auction listing.

- *Cash register.* If you have a retail operation, you need a way to track sales, collect money, and make change. You can do this with something as simple as a divided cash drawer and a printing calculator, or you can purchase a sophisticated, state-of-the-art point-of-sale system that is networked with your computer. Of course, the latter will cost somewhere between $1,200 and $5,000 per terminal and may not be a practical investment for a small start-up operation. A preferable option is an electronic cash register (ECR), which can range from $600 to $3,000 and can be purchased outright, leased, or acquired under a lease-purchase agreement. The newer ECRs offer such options as payment records to designate whether a customer paid by cash, check, or charge; department price groupings (appropriate for stores with multiple departments so you can separate the prices for items in each department); sign-in keys to help you monitor cashiers and clerks; and product price groups (which let you organize products as they are rung up) for tracking inventory more effectively.

- *Credit and debit card processing equipment.* This could range from a simple imprint machine to an online terminal. Credit and debit card service providers are widely available, so shop around to understand the service options, fees, and equipment costs. Expect to pay about $500 for a "swipe" machine that reads the magnetic strip on cards. You'll also pay a transaction charge, which might be a flat rate (perhaps 20 to 30 cents) per transaction or a percentage (typically 1.6 to 3.5 percent) of the sale. You'll probably pay higher transaction fees for internet sales, because the fraud risk the bank is accepting is higher than with face-to-face transactions.

PayPal, a subsidiary of eBay, is probably the most convenient and economical payment processing service available online (see Chapter 9). The majority of eBay buyers prefer to pay using PayPal because of the convenience as well as the Buyer's

Dollar Stretcher

Just about any type of second-hand business equipment can be purchased for a fraction of its original retail cost. In addition to shopping on eBay for used items, check the classified section of your local newspaper and ask new equipment dealers if they have trade-ins or repossessions for sale. Careful shopping for pre-owned items can save you hundreds of dollars.

▲

Protection Plan. Because of its popularity, many sellers—like Andrew Robinson of Boston Tables—who use different merchant accounts also offer PayPal as a payment choice.

Use the "Equipment and Supplies Shopping List" on page 125 to make sure you've considered every item you may need for your business. Remember, if you're on a budget, start small and acquire equipment and supplies as you grow. This may take some serious disci-

> **Bright Idea**
> If your storage space is limited, try negotiating a deal like this with your suppliers: Make a long-term purchase commitment to earn volume pricing, but arrange for delivery in increments so you don't have to store the goods.

pline on your part, especially in the beginning, but it will be worth it in the long run.

Vehicles

The largest single piece of equipment you'll need is a vehicle to take packages going out of the area to shipping companies such as the post office or UPS and for shopping expeditions. You need a reliable, fuel-efficient vehicle with sufficient cargo capacity. Some eBay sellers drive vans; others have found that smaller cars with fold-down back seats and hatchbacks are sufficient and easier to maneuver.

If the vehicle you presently own is suitable, using it—at least during the start-up process—will conserve your initial capital outlay. If it's not, or if you prefer to maintain a personal vehicle and a business vehicle, you'll have to lease or purchase one that will meet your needs. When you're ready to buy a vehicle, check eBay Motors before making a final decision.

Security

Whether you are homebased or in a retail or commercial warehouse location, remember that small merchandise, office equipment and cash attract burglars, robbers, and shoplifters. Not only do you need to protect your inventory and equipment with alarms, lighting, and a careful selection of employees, but you also need to secure your personal safety as well as that of your employees.

Begin by investigating your area's crime history to determine what kind of measures you need to take. To learn whether your proposed or existing location has a high crime rate, check with the local police department's community relations department or crime prevention officer. Most will gladly provide free information on safeguarding your business and will often even personally visit your site to discuss specific crime prevention strategies. Many also offer training seminars for small businesses and their employees on workplace safety and crime prevention.

Common techniques retailers use to enhance security and reduce shoplifting include mirrors, alarms, and video monitors. Technology is bringing the cost of these items down rapidly, and installing them may also earn you discounts on your insurance premiums. You can also increase the effectiveness of your security system by discreetly posting signs in your store windows and around the store announcing the presence of the equipment.

Sign Here

Contracts are an excellent tool to make sure both supplier and customer are clear on the details of the sale. Garriss says that one of his early mistakes that became a significant learning experience involved failing to get an adequate contract with a vendor. This is not "just a formality" that can be brushed aside. Read all agreements and support documents carefully, and consider having them reviewed by an attorney. Make sure everything that's important to you is in writing. Remember, if it's not part of the contract, it's not part of the deal—no matter what the other person says. And if it's in the contract, it's probably enforceable.

Any contract the vendor writes is naturally going to favor the vendor, but you don't have to agree to all the standard "boilerplate" terms. In addition, you can demand the inclusion of details that are appropriate to your specific situation. Consider these points when you're negotiating contracts:

○ *Make standard provisions apply to both parties.* If, for example, the contract exempts the vendor from specific liabilities, request that the language be revised to exempt you, too.

○ *Use precise language.* It's difficult to enforce vague language, so be specific. A clause that states the vendor is not responsible for failures due to "causes beyond the vendor's control" leaves a lot of room for interpretation; more precise language forces a greater level of accountability.

○ *Include a "vendor default" provision.* The vendor's contract probably describes the circumstances under which you would be considered to be in default; include the same protection for yourself.

○ *Be wary of vendor representatives who have to get any contract changes approved by "corporate" or some other higher authority.* This is a negotiating technique that generally works against the customer. Insist that the vendor make personnel with the authority to negotiate available.

Purchasing

No matter how smart a consumer you are, when it comes to business purchasing, you're playing a new game. The rules are different, and the stakes are significantly higher. But correctly done, purchasing—or procurement—will increase your net income.

Choosing Suppliers

Whether you're buying items to sell, a major piece of office equipment, or a toner cartridge for your laser printer, you should evaluate each vendor on quality, service, and price. Look at the product itself, as well as the supplemental services and support the company provides. And always check eBay before you make a final buying decision. "We always check eBay first, and we find some pretty good deals there," says Gotham City Online's Jonathan Garriss.

Verify the company's claims before making a purchase commitment. Ask for references and do a credit check on the vendor just as you would on a new customer. A credit check will tell you how well the supplier pays his own suppliers. This is particularly important for inventory sources because it could ultimately affect you. If your vendor is not paying his own vendors, he may have trouble getting materials, and that may delay delivery on your order(s). Or he may simply go out of business without any advance notice, leaving you in a lurch. Also confirm the company's general reputation and financial stability by calling the Better Business Bureau, any appropriate licensing agencies, trade associations, and D&B.

A major component of the purchasing process is the supplier's representative, or salesperson. The knowledge and sophistication level of individual salespeople often depends on the product or industry; however, they can be a tremendous source of education and information. Some businesspeople dismiss sales reps with an attitude of "I don't have time to see peddlers," but this is a mistake. Make it a rule to treat all salespeople with courtesy and respect, but insist that they do the same for you. You can, for example, set and enforce a policy that salespeople are seen only by appointment, or at certain hours. You can also ask them in advance how much time you need to allot for your meeting, and stick to that schedule.

Besides telling you what they have, salespeople should also be asking questions. A good salesperson will try to find out what your needs are and how his company can satisfy

Dollar Stretcher

Ask suppliers if payment terms can be a part of your price negotiation. For example, can you get a discount for paying cash in advance?

Equipment and Supplies Shopping List

Use the following checklist as a shopping guide to get your workspace and store (if you start a retail operation) set up. Each item listed is not necessarily required before you start, but you may want to have most of them eventually.

Computer and Office Equipment and Supplies

❑ Computer system (with printer)
❑ Digital camera
❑ Scanner
❑ Fax machine
❑ One- or two-line, full-featured phone system
❑ Voice mail
❑ E-mail
❑ Web site design
❑ Web site hosting
❑ Uninterruptible power supply
❑ Zip drive backup
❑ Surge protector
❑ Calculator
❑ Copier
❑ Desk
❑ Desk chair
❑ Printer stand
❑ File cabinet(s)
❑ Bookcase
❑ Computer/copier paper
❑ Business cards
❑ Letterhead paper and envelopes
❑ Address stamp or labels
❑ Extra printer cartridge
❑ Extra fax cartridge
❑ Zip drive disks
❑ Mouse pad
❑ Miscellaneous office supplies

Storage Fixtures and Hardware

❑ Storage shelves, cabinets

Store Equipment/Fixtures and Supplies (for retail operations)

❑ Special displays, related hardware
❑ Display shelving
❑ Cash register
❑ Counter
❑ Price marking equipment
❑ Floor gondolas
❑ Pegboard
❑ Hooks
❑ Showcases
❑ Wall gondolas

Retail Supplies

❑ Cash register tape
❑ Shopping bags
❑ Gift boxes
❑ Sales tags and/or labels

Shipping Equipment and Supplies

❑ Hand truck
❑ High-speed tape dispenser
❑ Carton stapler
❑ Postage scale
❑ Paper shredder
❑ Sealing tape
❑ Boxes
❑ Mailing labels
❑ Cushioned mailers
❑ Packing materials

Other Equipment

❑ Company vehicle
❑ Signage
❑ Security system

them. Just as in the consumer sales arena, commercial salespeople use both high- and low-pressure tactics. Consider studying sales techniques so you can recognize and respond to the methods being used on you.

Build Strong Supplier Relationships

Reliable suppliers are an asset to your business. They can bail you out when you make an ordering mistake or when your clients make difficult demands on you. But they will do so only as long as your business is profitable to them. Suppliers, like you, are in business to make money. If you argue over every invoice, ask them to shave prices on everything they sell you, or fail to pay your bills promptly, don't be surprised when their salespeople stop calling on you or refuse to help you when you're in a bind.

Of course, you want the best deal you can get on a consistent basis from your suppliers—this is just good business. Just keep in mind that no worthwhile business arrangement can continue for long unless something of value is rendered and received by all involved. The best approach is to treat your suppliers the way you would like each of your customers to treat you.

Find out in advance what your suppliers' credit policies are and pay according to their terms. Most will accept credit cards but will not put you on an open account until they've had a chance to run a credit check on you. They may ask you to provide a financial statement; if they do, don't even think of inflating your numbers to cover a lack of references. This is a felony, and it's easily detected by most credit managers.

If you do open an account with a supplier, be sure you understand their terms and preserve your credit score by paying on time. Typically, you'll have 30 days to pay, but many companies offer a discount if you pay early.

Customer
Service

Do you sometimes—or even often—feel that good customer service is a thing of the past? It may be in some business environments, but eBay is a different story. eBay customers demand—and enjoy—a high level of customer service, and if you're going to succeed selling on eBay, you need to take care of your buyers. Most of them know what they're looking for and have a good sense of its value, and they expect good service as part of the bargain.

Trappe, Maryland, PowerSeller Bob Willey says the best way to succeed in this business is to have a positive outlook and provide excellent customer service. "I have received only one negative feedback out of more than 4,700," he says. "I think that is because I do good, honest business, and most people appreciate that."

We asked eBay sellers what's different about customer service when you're selling on eBay as opposed to through other channels.

"It's much more intensive," says Gotham City Online's Jonathan Garriss. "[Bidders] ask a lot more questions, and there is a lot more hand-holding." Also, he notes that the procedures for completing a transaction (payment method, shipping issues, etc.) vary significantly among eBay sellers, "so you have to work very hard to convey your message of what to do next, and how to complete the order."

Thank You Card

In every package you send out, include a document of some sort (letter, packing slip, invoice, business card, etc.) that thanks your customers for their purchase and tells them what to do if they are not completely satisfied with their purchase. Take a look at the example below, which was provided by one of the eBay sellers we interviewed.

Thank You

Thank you for your purchase from {insert User ID or eBay store}. I hope you are pleased with your purchase. If there are no problems, please leave positive feedback so that I will know you have received your item and are satisfied. If you have any questions or concerns, please contact me right away at {insert e-mail address} and you will receive a prompt response.

It was a pleasure doing business with you!

An aspect unique to online auctions is the feedback system (discussed in Chapter 7), where both buyers and sellers can leave comments about one another that are visible to all other eBay users. Providing poor customer service puts you at risk of negative feedback, which could have a serious impact on your sales. While most eBay users are reasonable and honest with the way they use the feedback system, a few see it more as a weapon than a tool and threaten to leave negative feedback if they don't get the goods or services they want, whether or not their request is realistic. This is commonly referred to as "feedback extortion" by many eBay members, and eBay has a firm policy against it that can result in the user's account being suspended. Naturally, you should try to work with difficult customers as best you can, but don't let nasty customers intimidate you with the threat of negative feedback. Remember that if a buyer leaves you negative feedback, the eBay system allows you to post a response to it.

Some customers are difficult because that's their basic nature, but others may give you a hard time simply because they don't know any better. Garriss says it's important to keep in mind that eBay is one of the easiest ways to buy something on the internet, which means it attracts a lot of novice online shoppers. "But if you've never done an online transaction before, you get a little concerned, a little nervous," he notes. That's why communication immediately following the close of an auction and then throughout the remainder of the time it takes to process the sale is critical.

Try not to take it personally when customers are rude and excessively demanding. Not every transaction is going to go smoothly. The important thing to remember is to remain calm, cool, and professional. Book seller Peggy Webb in Sisters, Oregon, says the only regrettable experience she had on eBay was right after she started selling and had a very difficult customer. "I got mad and posted some feedback that I normally would not have [posted]," she says. So during the heat of the moment Peggy recommends sitting back, taking a deep breath, and waiting for it to pass.

Communication Is Key

As soon as an auction closes, send the winning bidder a notice that outlines how the transaction will proceed. If you need to calculate the shipping before they pay, do so promptly. Let them know when you receive their payment and when you plan to ship. Once you have shipped, let them know the package is on the way and provide tracking information if available. Tell them when you post feedback, and ask them to post feedback for you when they have received the product. If you don't hear from them after they've had time to examine the item, follow up with an e-mail asking if they are satisfied. If they leave you positive feedback, thank them and tell them you hope to do business with them again.

From the minute you post an auction, be prepared to respond to e-mails promptly. Remember, these are messages coming from potential customers or existing customers who may purchase again. Bob Willey says that although some listings will not generate inquiries, you can expect to receive and answer an average of two to three e-mails on items that are higher in demand, and even more queries if the auction has an international appeal. "You have to be very responsive," he says. "People on eBay tend to be anxious and don't like to wait around."

"I can't tell you how many times I've been shopping for something and saw an auction that interested me, but I wanted more information about the item before I placed a bid," says part-time seller Liz Baker in Oviedo, Florida. "It's great when the seller answers promptly. When they don't, I don't bid—and who knows, I might have been willing to pay more than the highest bidder if my question had been answered."

Dear Buyer...

Whether you use an auction management system through eBay, PayPal, or a third party, automation is a key to success when selling on eBay. Develop a standard e-mail notification that goes out to each winning bidder as soon as the auction closes. The following message is an example:

Dear Buyer,

Congratulations on winning the referenced auction! I prefer payment through PayPal but will accept money orders or personal checks (must clear first) that can be sent to the address below.

International buyers should contact me before sending payment at [insert your e-mail address] and include your shipping address. I will reply and provide the revised shipping cost for you to include with your total payment.

Please review my About Me page to view my policies regarding shipping, payment, feedback, and returns, and let me know if you have any questions. Thank you!

Regards,
[Your signature]
[Your User ID, mailing address, and e-mail address]

Seller, Protect Thyself

eBay offers the following tips for sellers to assure smooth, problem-free transactions:

- ○ Represent your merchandise fairly and accurately.
- ○ Respond promptly to buyer questions.
- ○ Review buyer feedback so you know something about the person you're selling to.
- ○ Include a clearly stated return policy in your listing.
- ○ Ship with a tracking number and insurance to help resolve disputes if a customer claims nondelivery or if an item is damaged in transit.
- ○ Keep your shipping receipts so you have proof of shipment.
- ○ Only ship items to the buyer's verified billing address.
- ○ Don't ship until you have verified payment, which means holding merchandise until checks clear.
- ○ Keep copies of any proof you have of your item's authenticity.
- ○ Use extra caution with international payments, revised shipping information, unknown or new buyers, and unusual bidding activity on an item.
- ○ Contact your buyer immediately after an auction ends to thank them for the purchase, provide any final pricing and payment information, and let them know how long you will wait for payment and when you will be shipping the merchandise after payment is received.
- ○ If you want to limit the bidders you will accept, be sure to clearly state that in your auction description. For example, you might say, "No bidders with negative feedback" or "New bidders with no feedback must contact the seller before bidding."

If you see a pattern in the types of questions you get asked, look for ways to answer them in your item description or on your About Me page. You can also develop standard responses that you can easily paste into an e-mail and quickly customize for the particular situation.

Treat all your communications with other eBay users as business correspondence, and remember that the structure, tone, and details of your e-mails are a strong reflection of your operation. Begin your e-mails with a salutation, write in complete sentences, end with a proper closing, and proofread and spellcheck; then proofread again before you hit "Send."

▲

> ## Bright Idea
>
> Never say "no" to a cus-
> tomer. When they ask for
> something you don't provide, offer
> them an alternative instead.

Baker shares a story that emphasizes the importance of proofreading, not just running spellcheck. In the past, PayPal allowed sellers to opt to accept credit cards, which involves an extra fee, or to only accept cash payments through the system, which is free. She was interested in bidding on an item with payment terms of "cash, e-checks, check or money orders," but the listing also mentioned PayPal. Baker wanted to use a credit card through PayPal, so she e-mailed the seller and asked if he accepted PayPal. He replied: "Yes, PayPal is a great way to pay, just with a credit card."

Baker bid on the item, won the auction, and paid as she planned, with a credit card through PayPal. The payment was immediately declined, and she received an e-mail from the seller that said, "Sorry, but I do not accept credit card payments. The fees are too much. This was explained on the auction site and again in the payment e-mail."

Baker went back to the original e-mail and sent it to the seller. He had left out one single word—*not*—which meant his message said the exact opposite of what he meant. "He meant to write that PayPal was fine, just not with a credit card," Baker says. "I ended up mailing him a personal check, but it was a hassle. It would have been so much easier if he had proofread his e-mail before he sent it."

(Note: eBay now requires all sellers to accept credit card payments through Pay-Pal or not accept PayPal at all.)

Providing Great Customer Service

Whether your business consists exclusively of auctions or you also sell from a web site or even a brick-and-mortar store, the basic principles of customer service remain the same:

- *See your business through your customers' eyes.* Is your operation user-friendly, efficient, and responsive? With their questions and high expectations, Garriss says eBay customers will force you to thoroughly understand your business processes.
- *Ask what your customers want and need.* Don't assume that you know what your customers want; ask them—and listen to their answers.
- *Meet or exceed expectations.* When you promise to do something—whether it's provide information, ship a product, or something else—do as you promised, or better.
- *Ask if there's anything else you can do.* When the transaction is complete, find out if you can provide any other product or service. A simple, "Is there anything

else I can help you with?" can net you additional sales and invaluable goodwill.

- *Keep in touch.* Let your customers know that they are important to you after the sale is complete and you've gotten their money.

- *Be a copycat.* Pay attention to good customer service when you receive it, whether it's in a restaurant, the grocery store, or elsewhere, and duplicate those techniques in your own operation.

Bright Idea

A great customer service technique that will also help increase sales in your eBay store is to offer free or discounted shipping on items a winning bidder might purchase from your store on the same day the auction they win closes.

Dealing with Nonpaying Bidders

When it comes to nonpaying bidders, give your customers the benefit of the doubt, at least in the beginning. Your auction listing should clearly state your payment terms. Typically, sellers ask that payment be made within three to ten days of the close of the auction, and most bidders do that because they're excited about their purchase and eager to receive the merchandise. When your auction closes, send the bidder an invoice with the final amount due (including shipping, handling, insurance, and any other charges that may apply) that clearly states when payment is due. You can do this through eBay, with your auction management software, or manually via e-mail.

Webb has written in her terms of service that she needs to receive payment within ten days. "But I don't want to sound like I'm standing over people with a baseball bat like some sellers do," she says. "That's a real turnoff." Instead, she prefers to dangle a carrot by promising good customer service and letting them know she will work with them in any way that she can. This policy has worked well for Webb because she rarely has to deal with the issue of a nonpaying bidder.

If you have not received payment by the due date, send a follow-up notice—but be nice about it. You can create your own notice, or use the standard payment reminder notice eBay provides (you'll see a button for that on the "Items I've Sold" section of your My eBay page). Consultant Paul Mladjenovic tells the story of winning an auction on eBay, but between the time he placed the winning bid and the time the auction closed, his mother was rushed to the hospital and spent several days in intensive care. He understandably forgot about making the payment. On the fourth day, he says, he received a nasty e-mail from the seller. He explained his situation to the seller and paid for the item promptly, and the seller apologized for the tone of the follow-up e-mail.

Bright Idea

Treat your customers like gold—because they are!

Clearly, it would have been better all the way around had the seller's follow-up note been a gentle reminder with a request for communication if there was a reason for payment not being made.

Of course, you will encounter bidders who are unable to pay or who change their minds after winning a bid and decide to default on the auction contract. Antiques dealer Sue Rudolph in Winter Park, Florida, recalls being strung along for weeks by a buyer who kept asking for a little more time to pay for an item. She never paid, and Rudolph ended up having to relist the item and file for a credit on her final value fee for the completed auction item that was never paid for. This is the type of bidder you'll want to put on your blocked bidder list (explained in Chapter 7).

When a bidder doesn't pay in the amount of time you stipulate in your terms and does not respond to payment reminders, you are free to relist the item and sell it to someone else. You should also file a nonpaying bidder alert and request a credit on your

Sample Return Policy

The following is a sample return policy and may give you a few ideas on how you might want to word yours:

We want our customers to be happy, which is why we provide a 30-day, no-questions-asked, money-back guarantee on all products. If for any reason you are not satisfied with your purchase, notify us by e-mail or phone, and we will promptly issue a Return Merchandise Authorization (RMA). Any item listed as "all sales final" will not be accepted for return, and no refund or credit will be issued. Shipping charges are not refundable unless the return is due to our error.

To assist us in expediting your return, exchange, and/or refund, we ask that you:

❑ Contact us prior to returning the merchandise.

❑ Return the merchandise to us within 30 days of the date you received it.

❑ Return products in their original packaging in resaleable condition.

❑ Include all accessories.

❑ Include a copy of the invoice and/or packing slip.

❑ Mark the RMA number clearly on the outside of the box so we can easily identify your package when it arrives and handle your return promptly.

Refunds are made in the same form as your payment and will be issued within seven days of our receipt of the returned merchandise. If your payment was made by personal check, your refund will be held until we can confirm that your check has cleared. You may elect to receive credit instead of a refund.

final value fee for that transaction. You may file a nonpaying bidder alert at least seven days but no more than 45 days after your auction closes. To file a nonpaying bidder alert, go to "Help," search for "nonpaying bidder," and follow the instructions.

Establish a Return and Refund Policy

Decide how you're going to deal with returns, and state that policy clearly in all your auctions. If your return policy requires in-depth explanation, provide this on your About Me page.

Your return policy should include a time limit, a description of the circumstances under which items can be returned, who pays for shipping (Will you refund shipping costs if an item is returned? Most sellers don't.), whether or not you charge a restocking fee, and any procedures customers must follow to return an item. If your return policy promises to make refunds to dissatisfied customers, you are required by federal law to do that.

"I've had to issue refunds a few times, but it doesn't happen often," says Laurie Ayers. "I'm not going to argue with people too much. If they are not happy, they can send it back and I'll issue a refund." She will also consider a partial refund if the customer isn't totally satisfied but is willing to keep the merchandise.

Being reasonable, even when the customer is in the wrong, can pay off. Part-time eBay seller Susan Marler in Selma, North Carolina, auctioned a Sprint Nokia cell phone, and the winning bidder wanted to send the phone back because she thought it would work with her AT&T service provider, but it didn't. Though Marler would have been within her rights to refuse to accept the return because she had described it accurately and the bidder made the error, she says, "I agreed to let her send it back and give her a refund minus shipping paid. She thought about it and decided to keep it and sell it herself on eBay."

David Lynn in San Diego says Combined Direct has a satisfaction-guaranteed policy. Depending on the value of the product, they sometimes will not require the customer to ship it back. "If it's a higher-dollar item and something we expect to get back in a saleable condition, we'll ask them to send it back," he says. Although Combined Direct gives a full refund, under certain circumstances the company will ask the customer to pay for return shipping—such as if the buyer didn't read the description correctly and got the wrong color or measurements.

Problems with Your Drop-Shipper

If you are selling new products purchased through a distributor who drop-ships for you and something arrives with a factory defect or damage, it is the distributor's responsibility

▲

to handle the problem. However, your customer didn't buy from the distributor; he bought from you. So you need to stay involved until the situation is resolved.

You should already know your distributor's return policy, so when you find out about a defective product (and for internet sales, that news will usually come via e-mail), you should simply follow the steps your distributor requires. Typically, you'll contact the distributor, explain the problem, get a return merchandise authorization, and ask them to arrange to have the product picked up. Then you'll e-mail your customer with the RMA number and instructions for the return (such as repackaging the product in the original box, writing the RMA number on the outside of the box, and coordinating the pickup). Your distributor should also replace the defective product at no additional charge to you or your customer.

SquareTrade

SquareTrade is a great eBay tool to reduce the risk of problems with transactions. By displaying the SquareTrade seal on your auctions, you are demonstrating a level of trustworthiness, and buyers will feel confident that they will have a positive experience dealing with you. For a small monthly fee, SquareTrade offers buyer protection services, negative feedback notification, dispute resolution, and more.

Recently, SquareTrade has branched out to include in its services something called SideBar, a desktop toolbar that interacts as a shopping assistant for its users by providing competitive price comparisons on eBay, as well as other online sites. This tool also includes anti-phishing and fraud detection technology that alerts users if they click on a suspicious link.

For additional information, check out eBay's SquareTrade section by clicking on the "Services" link at the top of eBay's home page, and then clicking on "Buying & Selling."

Common Auction Scams

While it's not specifically a customer service issue, you should still understand the common scams that occur in the auction world, be able to recognize them, and know what to do if you believe it's happening in one of your auctions. Though eBay works hard to maintain the integrity of the auction process, unscrupulous people will always try to circumvent the rules to increase their profits. All the following scams are against eBay policies:

Bid Shielding

Bid shielding is when someone uses a secondary user ID or has another eBay member bid on an item to raise the bidding to an extremely high level, and then that high bid is retracted at the last minute, and the low bid level of another bidder is protected. An example would look like this: Mary puts a necklace and earring set up for auction; the set is reasonably worth $35. Susan bids $20 and then asks Kathy to bid $50 to scare away other bidders. Kathy places her bid but at the last minute retracts it. Because no one else has bid, Susan gets the jewelry at her bid of $20. eBay's proxy bidding system and policies on bid retractions make bid shielding difficult, but enterprising scammers will still try to do it.

Shill Bidding

Shill bidding has plagued legitimate auctions since they began in ancient Rome. In a traditional auction, a person known as a shill will place bids to drive up the price of an item and then back off and let another bidder win the auction when the price is sufficiently high. The same thing can happen in an online auction; someone places bids to artificially raise the price of an item.

eBay users might participate in shill bidding, either in an effort to generate interest in their own auction or to help a friend. Don't do this type of insincere bidding; it could result in being suspended from eBay. To avoid even the appearance of being involved in shill bidding, eBay recommends that family members,

> **Beware!**
> Although eBay makes every effort to protect its users from fraud, it is not totally impossible for a hacker to penetrate the system (whether eBay or another auction site) and steal personal financial information. Be cautious when revealing your information, and check your bank and credit card statements carefully.

friends, and individuals who live together, work together, or share a computer not bid on each other's items. Even though eBay benefits from shill bidding because higher sale prices mean higher final value fees, buyers will be reluctant to bid if they suspect shill bidding, and that is ultimately not good for eBay as a company as well as the entire online auction community.

In addition to being against eBay's policies, shill bidding is illegal in many jurisdictions and can result in criminal prosecution.

False Testimonials

Some sellers have been known to create fake user IDs so they can place glowing testimonials about themselves in the feedback section of eBay and in the comment section of other auction sites.

This type of feedback shilling can also work in reverse if an eBay member wants to damage another user's account by leaving them negative feedback. In addition to being unethical, this type of activity is fraudulent.

Counterfeit Money Orders

In this scam, the seller receives a legitimate-looking money order in the amount requested and sends out the item before depositing the money order, only to discover later that the bank will not honor it because it's a fake. The best course of action is to cash the money order and wait a few days before mailing out the item.

Another scam along the same lines is when a buyer sends you a fake money order in an amount much larger than the winning bid. The buyer asks you to send the item and remaining balance to their friend or family member at another address (usually in a foreign country and impossible to recover). By the time the bank notifies you of the problem, you have already deposited the money order and sent out the product and monies as instructed. This means you lose the item, shipping costs, and hard-earned cash. If you ever receive a money order like this, immediately notify eBay's security team, which will help you take appropriate action.

The bottom line is to always confirm that you are in receipt of the actual funds before shipping merchandise.

Chargebacks

Some scammers will pay you with a credit card service and then, after you've shipped the goods, they'll initiate a chargeback to take the money out of your account, claiming they did not receive the shipment. You can avoid this problem by insuring your packages and by requesting a delivery confirmation on all packages that you send out.

The Value of Repeat Business

In an ideal world, every sale would be equally profitable. But you're not going to be selling in an ideal world, and you need to recognize that for most companies, subsequent sales are generally more profitable than the initial sale, which is why you should have a system in place to encourage repeat business.

"We make it as easy and as safe for people to shop with us on eBay as we possibly can," says Jonathan Garriss. Gotham City Online features great pictures, thorough product descriptions, and a liberal return policy. The company accepts virtually all forms of payment. "People get very comfortable with us, and it results in repeat customers and great word-of-mouth publicity. It's very beneficial for your business."

Peggy Webb says that she has several repeat customers. "I like to leave them special feedback so they will know they were recognized and feel welcome."

"The single toughest thing to do in the world of business is to get a customer the first time around," says consultant Paul Mladjenovic. Once you've got that customer—by answering e-mails promptly, providing a quality product and great customer service, following up as necessary and appropriate, etc.—take advantage of the fact that they know you and trust you, and sell to them again.

Inventory, Storage, and Shipping

Now we're ready to tackle some more of the nuts and bolts of running an eBay business: inventory, storage, and shipping.

Inventory and Storage

Regardless of the size of your operation, accurate inventory maintenance and tracking is critical. You need to know what's on order, what's on its way to you, what you have on hand, and what's been shipped. Small part-time eBay sellers can do that manually, sometimes even by just doing a quick visual check of the area where they store their inventory. But if you're going to grow, you need a system, and the best and easiest time to put that system in place is when you're getting started.

A companion issue to tracking your inventory is how and where you store it. Storage is a key issue for eBay sellers. If you have adequate storage space, you can buy at great prices off-season and sell when those items will go for the greatest profits. If your storage space is limited, you'll have to be more selective about what you maintain in inventory.

Another issue to consider about storage is the quality of the environment. Is it air conditioned? Dry? Free of odors (especially cigarette smoke, but even household and pet odors) that might be absorbed by your merchandise?

Sue Rudolph, the antiques dealer in Winter Park, Florida, stores her inventory in a specially outfitted closet in her computer room. As a part-time seller, when she wants to list something, she just opens the closet, studies her inventory and makes a selection.

Tip...

Smart Tip
Keeping unsold inventory on hand is expensive and a waste of space. If something hasn't sold in a reasonable time—Laurie Ayers will give it two chances in an auction—get rid of it.

Though still small, Laurie Ayers is a higher-volume seller. She has shelving units in her office marked "to be listed," "listed," and "closed, waiting payment." She moves items from one area to the next as appropriate. "I try to send things out the day I receive payment, so I don't have a 'paid, to be shipped' shelf," she says.

eBay PowerSeller and Trading Assistant Bob Willey also uses a shelving system in the 700-square-foot space he has dedicated to his eBay business. "In this area I have a shelving inventory system with ten units, each of which holds four to five shelves," he says. Willey says the plastic units hold up well, work with most any type of décor, and can be purchased inexpensively at a local discount store such as Wal-Mart. But to keep track of his inventory, he uses an auction management system.

To track your own inventory, use auction management software, spreadsheets, or even index cards—whatever simplifies the process for you and works best. Part-time Oviedo, Florida, seller Liz Baker keeps tabs on her books and other items by using an Excel spreadsheet; however, she plans to upgrade to a book inventory software system in the near future.

Clearly, it's possible to earn a respectable income selling on eBay and using manual inventory management methods. But if you're going to build a business based on technology (selling on the internet), why not go all the way and use technology to track and maintain your inventory?

"Probably the most important aspect of having an online business is being able to manage your inventory in a nonmanual way," says Jonathan Garriss. At any given time, Gotham City Online has thousands of items in inventory, all tracked by a sophisticated, customized system.

Garriss recalls talking to an eBay shoe seller who typically stocks anywhere from 500 to 600 pairs of shoes at a time and tracks her inventory with yellow sticky notes. He says she spends an average of six hours a day writing those notes and trying to find items. Inventory management software could cut that to literally minutes. Another point to keep in mind is that many auction management software programs and services include an inventory management element.

If you're selling collectibles, used items, merchandise you pick up at garage sales, etc., you will have to maintain and track those items in your inventory. However, if you're going to buy wholesale to resell, you have two options: You can buy in large quantities and store the goods until you sell them, or you can buy from distributors who will drop-ship your merchandise to your customers, and you can avoid the hassle of maintaining any inventory. We discussed the drop-shipping process in Chapter 6 as it relates to stocking your eBay store; it can also work well with auctions, other types of internet sales, and mail order.

Shipping

In most eBay transactions, the buyer pays for shipping, but that doesn't mean you don't have to worry about handling this part of the transaction effectively and efficiently. Because shipping can add substantially to the bottom-line cost of an item for bidders, many eBay sellers focus on products that are small, easy to pack, and don't cost a lot to ship.

Tustin, California, eBay seller Linda Parker set up a packing and shipping station in the garage of her Tustin, California, home to make this part of eBay selling faster and more efficient. Other homebased eBay sellers have taken similar steps, realizing that spending an excessive amount of time on packing and shipping has a negative impact on your overall profit picture.

Many eBay sellers say one of their biggest early mistakes was underestimating shipping charges. If you are setting a fixed shipping price in your auction (which is more and more difficult to do fairly and accurately, since rates vary so much according to the package's destination), be sure you calculate it accurately. Susan Marler in

Selma, North Carolina, sold an item for $8 plus shipping. But the shipping cost she estimated in her auction was $4 less than what it actually turned out to be, which seriously eroded her profit on the sale. Many sellers are now asking buyers to e-mail them their address when the auction ends so that they can calculate exact shipping charges to that address instead of setting a fixed, ballpark shipping cost in each auction. Although it's sometimes more work to do it this way (the seller has to calculate exact shipping charges on each and every package), buyers often appreciate knowing that they aren't paying more than what it actually costs the seller to ship the item to them. A decent postage scale is essential so you can quote accurate shipping charges. See Chapter 11 for more on scales.

If you choose to set fixed shipping prices, when you're writing your auction description, go ahead and weigh the item while you have it out and in your hands. Then add a pound or so (depending on how large and/or fragile it is) for packing materials. It's also reasonable to add a small charge to cover the cost of your packing materials. However, be fair with your shipping and handling charges. Certainly cover

It's All in the Technique

Some items require special packing attention, such as:

○ *Artwork.* Use cartons specially designed for artwork, and use generous amounts of bubble wrap and cushioning material. Items that are of very high value or are particularly awkward in shape should be professionally packed or crated. Remove glass from framed artwork and pack separately.

○ *High-value coins, stamps, and jewelry.* In addition to packing to protect the contents, use larger-than-necessary boxes to reduce the risk of the package being lost or stolen.

○ *China and glassware.* Double-box whenever practical. All pieces should be individually wrapped in clean paper or tissues. Add a 2- to 3-inch layer of crumpled paper or other cushioning between the items and inner wall of the carton. Cups, dishes, saucers, and shallow bowls should be placed in the carton on edge. Deep bowls, glasses, and serving vessels should be placed in the carton with their rims toward the bottom of the carton. Fill the center of hollow items, such as vases, with paper to make them more solid.

○ *Electronics.* When shipping televisions, computers, stereo systems, and other electronic devices, use the original cartons and packing, if possible. If not, use anti-static bubble wrap and lots of cushioning materials.

your costs, but resist the urge to make this a profit center. Experienced buyers will recognize that you're trying to make a profit on the shipping part of the sale, and they might not buy from you because of it.

"People don't mind paying a little more for shipping when the item is fragile and you're going to the time and expense of packing it well and double-boxing it," says Rudolph.

> **Bright Idea**
>
> Offer customers a choice in shipping methods: basic, low-cost ground, plus same-day, next-day, or second-day air service if they need the item in a hurry and are willing to pay for that privilege.

While that may be true, Paul Mladjenovic tells of the time he bought a CD for $1.99. "I confess that I didn't read the entire listing, and that would have made a difference. But I really wanted the information, and the organization that sent it to me charged me $12 for shipping, handling, and insurance." The CD arrived in a simple envelope with a postage stamp, and Mladjenovic felt he had been seriously gouged by the seller.

"Are there times when you can reasonably charge more than the price of the item for shipping and handling? Yes. If I'm selling a brick and you're buying it for $1, it's going to cost a lot more than that to ship it. But people understand that," Mladjenovic says. "So you've got to put [all the shipping-related costs] into the description. Otherwise, people might feel they were cheated. And on eBay, if [someone feels like you have cheated them], they are going to put a negative feedback rating in place, and that's your reputation."

When calculating shipping charges, be sure to keep the density of your item in mind. Very light, bulky items are likely to be subject to dimensional weight charges— that is, you have to pay for the space your shipment is taking up rather than the weight. Carriers use a standard formula to calculate dimensional weight based on the measurements of the package, and you pay based on the actual weight or the dimensional weight, whichever is more.

Remember the adage "underpromise and overdeliver"; give yourself some wiggle room on your delivery commitments in case a situation comes up that is out of your control. For instance, deliveries may be delayed due to inclement weather. Sometimes packages are sent to the wrong address because the buyer neglected to update their eBay or PayPal account.

Without a doubt, shipping is a functional necessity, and it can be a disaster waiting to happen. But it can also be a marketing tool. Offer choices so your customers can select how fast they want to receive their merchandise and how much they want to pay. Consider offering free shipping on big items, Buy It Now items, or multiple purchases, or combine shipping on several small items.

If potential bidders send you e-mails asking how much shipping will cost for one of your auction items, have them send you their ZIP code, and then use the postage calculators at www.usps.com or www.ups.com (or whatever carrier you're considering using) to figure the exact cost. Another alternative is to insert the eBay shipping calculator in your auctions. That way, potential bidders can figure the shipping costs themselves and not have to send you an e-mail and wait for your reply.

Whenever possible, include the cost of shipping in your auction description so prospective buyers can take that into consideration when placing a bid. Georgene Harkness of My New Threads in Plano, Texas, prefers to ship her clothing items via Priority Mail and charge her clients a flat fee. "This way, they don't have to figure out what it's going to cost or send me an e-mail," she says.

For large, bulky items, you can use the free freight estimator found at http://ebay.freightquote.com.

Packing

Good packing is essential to protect your merchandise while it's in transit. Remember that your packages are going to be on a truck with other packages, they'll probably be loaded and unloaded several times, they'll likely experience bumps and vibrations, they may have other boxes stacked on top of them, and they may get dropped (or tossed around) repeatedly. All the "fragile" stickers in the world won't protect a carelessly packed shipment from damage.

Andrew Robinson of Boston Tables says sellers can eliminate problems before they occur with proper packaging. "So many people don't understand what can happen to heavy products that are shipped across the country," he says. "To mitigate potential damages, we have designed and customized our own crates and shipping materials to protect our products."

While you probably won't need to construct your own shipping materials, your best line of defense against freight damage is to pack your items to travel safely. Heed these tips:

- Use only sturdy cartons that can be completely sealed. Corrugated boxes are usually best.
- Pack firmly, but don't overload the box. Cartons should not rattle or bulge.

- Maintain a padded space between your item and the wall of the box to absorb shocks.
- Each item should be wrapped individually in paper or cloth and separated from other items with sufficient cushioning to prevent damage from shock or vibration.
- Pack items in layers, placing the heaviest items on the bottom and the lightest on top.
- Do not pack hard or heavy items in the same box with fragile items.
- Seal each box completely with appropriate packaging tape. Don't use duct tape, electrical tape, cellophane tape, or masking tape on your packages. These tapes might be great for a variety of other functions, but they're not good for securing packages—they tend to peel off and/or deteriorate during transit. Do not use string; it can get caught in automated sorting equipment and damage both the equipment and your package. Paper over-wrap is discouraged for the same reason.
- Label each carton with the name and address of both the shipper and the recipient. Number the boxes in the case of multicarton shipments (example: Box 1 of 2, Box 2 of 4, etc.).

The Best Things in Life Are Free

Let everyone know that you'll take packing materials off their hands. Linda Parker says her husband's co-workers routinely save sturdy boxes, foam peanuts, and bubble wrap for her. "Packing materials are expensive, especially when you wrap a lot of glass like I do," she says. "So I appreciate my friends and my husband's associates keeping me stocked with this stuff."

Laurie Ayers gets large quantities of free bubble wrap from a local furniture store. "I have a friend who works there, and she gave me a heads-up on it," she says. "It's amazing what you can get for free when you ask. Companies that receive picture frames and other large fragile items get lots of packaging materials, and all they do is throw it away. So a few times a year, I go to my friend's store, fill up the back of my Jeep, and I'm good for months."

A great source of free shredded paper is your local post office. Your local postmaster may be willing to provide you with shredded nonsensitive returned mail to use as packing material. Another source of inexpensive paper filler is the end rolls of newsprint that are available from your local newspaper; often these are free or available for a nominal charge.

- Include an inside label with complete shipper and recipient names and addresses in case anything happens to the outside label and it can't be read.

- Many shipping experts recommend using only new boxes, but eBay sellers routinely reuse boxes with satisfactory results. If you are reusing a box, be sure it's in good condition, and remove any old labels and shipment markings.

- If you are buying new merchandise from a manufacturer or wholesaler, consider having them pack your merchandise so it's ready for you to ship out rather than in bulk. You'll have to pay extra, but you'll save on in-house labor and supplies.

> **Tip...**
>
> **Smart Tip**
>
> Many package carriers (USPS, FedEx, UPS, and DHL, to name a few) provide packaging materials for certain service levels for free. The USPS, for example, provides free boxes for Express and Priority Mail shipments; however, it is against the law to use those boxes for any other purpose. Ask carriers what they provide and what restrictions apply.

Choosing a Carrier

There is a wide range of differences in the pricing and service levels of various package and freight carriers, and it's a good idea to become familiar with them before making a decision on which carrier to use. Customers will view your choice of carrier and the service they provide as an extension of your operation, so it's important to use one that delivers a high level of customer service and reliability. Don't make your decision based on cost alone; as important as price is, the lowest price is not always the best value.

It's important to understand the difference between a package carrier and a common carrier. Package carriers (such as UPS, FedEx, DHL, and USPS) handle smaller shipments with per-package weight limits typically ranging from 70 to 150 pounds. Many offer a choice of ground or air service. Common carriers are truck lines that handle large, heavy shipments that are too big for the package carriers.

When choosing a carrier, points to consider include:

- What are the size and weight limitations, and how does that compare with what you are shipping?

- What levels of service are available?

- Does the carrier offer online package tracking? How easy or difficult is it to use?

- Will the carrier make multiple delivery attempts without charging an extra fee?

- Does the carrier offer e-mail notification to let your customer know the package is on the way?

- Does the carrier deliver on Saturdays and, if so, is there an extra charge?

- How late will the carrier make pickups at your facility, and how does this blend with your work schedule?

- Does the carrier have a facility where your customers can pick up their package? (This is known as "hold for pickup.")

- Does the carrier offer return services to help you retrieve packages if necessary?

- Will the carrier provide delivery confirmation and, if so, is there an extra charge?

- Is the carrier financially stable?

Carrier selection is important not only for what you are shipping out but also for what you receive. If you are paying the freight on your incoming materials, you have the right to name the carrier. Beyond that, as a matter of good customer service, your suppliers should be willing to honor your carrier choice.

International Shipping

Many eBay sellers don't like to ship overseas because they don't understand the process or find it to be too much work. But if you take the time to learn how to do it—and for most countries, it's not complicated—you can increase your profits significantly.

Ayers says being willing to ship internationally gives her an edge over sellers who won't do it. "International people often don't have as many options, and if they're looking for something in particular, chances are they will bid higher," she says. "They pay the shipping, and the rates vary depending on the country. [Shipping to] some countries doesn't cost much more than shipping within the States, and to some the rates are ridiculous. I've had customers spend $40, $60, and more on shipping, but it was the only way they could get the item, so they were willing to pay."

Beware!

Never just sign a delivery receipt for packages. Even though you'll get to know your regular driver, always count the packages and do a quick visual inspection for external signs of damage.

Sisters, Oregon, eBay seller Peggy Webb says that after three years of selling on eBay, she finally got brave enough to offer international shipping and says that sales have increased somewhat. "A lot of what I offer is not available anywhere else except in the United States," she says. "International buyers are very excited when they find ordinary things that we take for granted. Plus, it has been really interesting talking to people from around the world."

Bright Idea

Reusing old cartons for shipping? You can make them look new with mask-out paint, a colored spray paint that dries instantly and will accept your own labels and tape. This product is available through most shipping supply sources.

David Lynn, IT director for San Diego–based CRI, says his company does a fair amount of international business in Canada, Puerto Rico, and occasionally Asia. "If they are willing to pay for the shipping costs," he says, "we'll send it anywhere."

The package and freight companies that deliver overseas (USPS, UPS, FedEx, DHL, etc.) have plenty of information to help you understand the procedures and paperwork necessary to ship to various international destinations. Contact the individual companies, or visit their web sites for details.

Insurance

Insurance protects you and your customers by paying to replace or repair items that are damaged in transit. For high-end or very fragile merchandise, insist that your buyers pay for insurance for the full value of the goods. For low-end or very sturdy merchandise, you may allow buyers to make the choice of whether or not to buy insurance. But stress that if they reject insurance, your responsibility ends with shipping. Be sure you can prove that you shipped the merchandise, either by using a carrier (such as UPS or FedEx) that will provide you with a shipper's receipt, or by using the USPS' delivery confirmation service.

Some carriers automatically provide coverage for loss or damage up to $100 per shipment at no extra charge; others charge for the first dollar of insurance coverage. Don't bother to buy insurance for more than you can prove the item is worth; the carrier will only reimburse you for the actual value, not for the amount of insurance you purchased. Documents that are generally accepted as proof of value include a current bill of sale, an invoice, or a statement from a certified appraiser.

Even when you purchase insurance, it's important that your items be properly packed for transit. If damage occurs and the carrier determines that the shipment was not appropriately packed, your claim (or the buyer's claim, in most cases) will likely be denied.

Some sellers prefer to "self-insure" packages, which is fine if you are guaranteeing delivery and willing to pay for damages out of your own pocket. However, be aware that many states have regulations about offering insurance and require an individual to be licensed, bonded, etc. What this means is that you cannot charge a separate insurance fee if you are self-insuring.

Delivery Confirmation

You can significantly decrease the risk of buyers claiming they never received a package by using USPS' delivery confirmation. This inexpensive service can give you peace of mind while tracking the shipment of packages across the country. Rates are typically lower—and sometimes free—for sellers who purchase postage electronically. However, note that while delivery confirmation is used to verify delivery of auction goods, it does not insure packages against damage.

Prompt Shipping Is the Law

The FTC's rules for mail and telephone order merchandise also apply to orders placed over the internet. You must have a reasonable basis for stating that a product can be shipped within a certain time. If you have the item in your inventory, that's usually not going to be a problem. But if you are depending on drop-shippers, you should be sure they are reliable. When you use a drop-shipper, you as the seller are responsible for complying with the law.

If your auction doesn't clearly state a shipment period, you must ship within 30 days of receiving the order. If you can't, you must notify the customer of the delay, provide a revised shipment date, and explain his right to cancel and get a full and prompt refund. Complete details of these federal rules, including detailed instructions for delay notifications, can be found at www.ftc.gov.

Marketing

Marketing is something many people don't like to do, but it can be as creative and as much fun as putting up and monitoring your auctions—and it's essential to the success of any business. The basic principles you'll use in marketing your business when you sell on eBay are the same as when you sell through any other channel. The most important thing to keep in mind about marketing is this: It's not an expense; it's an investment in your business.

Keep these questions in mind as you form your marketing plan:

- Who are your potential customers?
- How many of them are there?
- Where are they located?
- Whom are they buying from now?
- Can you offer them anything their current supplier is not providing?
- How do you compare with your competitors?
- What kind of image do you want your company to project?

The goal of your marketing plan should be to convey your existence and the quality of your service to prospective customers, ideally using a multifaceted approach.

Marketing Ideas That Work

Even though millions of people browse eBay every day, there's no guarantee that they're going to look at or bid on your auctions. That's why you need to be proactive in your efforts to get their attention.

Advertise

You may want to invest in advertising your auctions. This is an especially good idea when you have high-ticket items with substantial profit margins. Very few eBay sellers advertise their auctions outside eBay.

If you're going to go this route, choose a publication with a national circulation (such as *The Wall Street Journal*, *USA Today*, or *The New York Times*) and run a small classified or display ad in the appropriate section that describes what you're auctioning and includes the URL to locate the items on eBay.

The Element of Scarcity

One of the most powerful sales motivators is scarcity—that is, tapping into a bidder's fear that if he doesn't win this item right now, he'll never have a chance to acquire this item again. In your promotional materials—your listings, your own web site, your About Me page on eBay, your advertisements—use this tool whenever possible.

Be creative. Don't just say "Due to a limited supply, we are allowing only five widgets per customer." That's been overdone, and most people recognize it for what it is. Try something like "Due to unusual weather conditions in the region where our suppliers are located, we don't know when we will get another shipment of these items at this price, so get yours now."

Cross-Promote

eBay provides its sellers with the ability to cross-promote at no extra charge. Whenever a bidder bids on or wins one of your auctions, four of your other listings are promoted in a display box (they appear on the page the bidder/buyer is looking at). eBay will automatically select listings for you, or you can choose specific listings yourself. You can change and keep track of your cross-promotions from the "Items I'm Selling" view in My eBay.

Also, eBay has recently added another free cross-promotional tool called "Cross Promotion Connections." The idea behind this feature is to cross-promote your auctions with another seller's products that complement—but do not compete with—yours. For instance, if you sell sports clothing and another seller's niche is sports memorabilia, the two of you may decide to "connect" by issuing each other an invitation to join forces. Then, when a buyer bids on or wins one of your auctions, at the bottom of the notification page (following your own cross-promoted items) will be a display of similar items from that seller or other sellers with whom you are cross-promoting. Likewise, your auctions will show up on their bidder notification pages.

In addition to using these cross-promotional tools, each of your auction listings should also promote another listing and give the bidder a reason to check out your other auctions—including your store if you have one. At the very least, suggest that the bidder take a look at your other items—the link eBay provides ("View seller's other items") makes it easy. To be more sophisticated, insert your own link using HTML, and make a specific pitch. For example, "If you like this necklace, you'll love the earrings I'm selling, and I'll combine shipping if you win both auctions." Jonathan Garriss of Gotham City Online offers free shipping on any purchase from their eBay store and promotes that message in all their auction listings, which pulls in new and repeat buyers.

Keep an Eye on the Calendar

Make your auctions relative to the calendar. Tie your listings into upcoming holidays or seasonal events. If you're selling seasonal items, such as Christmas ornaments or Halloween decorations, a good rule of thumb is to note when retail stores are putting their holiday products on display. When you see theirs on the shelves, then it's probably time to start promoting yours.

eBay Keywords

eBay Keywords is a powerful marketing tool that directs browsers to your auction listings or eBay store. Whenever specific keywords or phrases are typed in, banner or text ads are prominently displayed at the top of the search results page. These unobtrusive ads are comparable to caller ID, as the user can glance at the title and description and make a quick assessment as to whether or not to pass or click the link for more information. These types of ads are generally well-received because when a user is looking for a specific product or service, the ads only appear when particular keywords or phrases are typed in.

This is a pay-per-click system that allows you to decide how much you are willing to pay when someone clicks your banner or text ad. For example, you decide how much you are willing to pay for a keyword or phrase each time a user clicks your ad. Naturally, the more you are willing to pay, the higher your ad will rank in the rotation for that selected keyword, because other sellers will also be jockeying for a position to place their ad using the same keyword. It is important to note that you are only charged when someone clicks on your ad—not every time it appears on a search results page. It is a competitive marketing tool that Trappe, Maryland, eBay entrepreneur Bob Willey uses with success. For more information, go to www.admarketplace.net.

Signature Lines

This simple marketing technique is one of the best marketing tools on the internet—and one of the most overlooked. Your e-mail and discussion board signature line is the perfect spot for an unobtrusive promotional pitch—almost like a virtual business card. Keep it short with no more than two to three lines that include a link to your eBay store, About Me page, or auction listings page. Add a plug about free shipping or highlight a special auction that you're running.

Write Great Descriptions

We discussed the importance of good item descriptions in Chapter 5, but the issue cannot be stressed too strongly. With an online auction or internet sale, you do not have the opportunity for face-to-face interaction where you can see your customer's expression, nor does your customer have the opportunity to actually see your merchandise. Write item descriptions that will work hard for you. Here's an excellent example: In a listing for a candy dish, an eBay seller described the dish in great detail, including meas-

> **Bright Idea**
>
> If your storage area is smoke-free, mention that when writing your auction listing. That is often a big selling point for nonsmokers.

urements, color, and design, and then added, "This dish holds a 13-ounce bag of Hershey's kisses." How much easier it was for a shopper to see that dish in her own home filled with chocolates!

Search Engine Optimization

eBay is constantly updating its site and developing new tools to help sellers boost their search engine optimization results. This strat-

> **Beware!**
> Even if everything you put in your auction description is true, if you leave out something important, your ad could be seen as misleading and subject to action by the FTC.

egy increases your chances of having your eBay pages show up when potential buyers conduct keyword searches on search engines like Yahoo! or Google.

Because it takes a while for the web crawlers to find new pages, search engine optimization will not be beneficial for short-term auction listings. However, eBay store listings, About Me pages, and submissions to Reviews and Guides (see below) that have all been optimized with relevant keywords and phrases can give you greater visibility to potential buyers.

For example, use significant keywords in your store description and categories. Sprinkle them throughout your About Me page, as it also gets indexed by the search engines. Because your About Me page is automatically updated by eBay with new listings, web crawlers will revisit this page more often because they see new content has been added, so be sure to provide links to your eBay store or non-eBay web site.

Unfortunately, you can't create your own title and description tags on your eBay pages, as these are managed by eBay. However, you can take advantage of eBay's search engine optimization tools on your own web site by providing links to your eBay store or About Me page that use specific keywords or phrases related to a product or category.

When thinking about what keywords to use, remember some of the search strategies discussed in Chapter 4. Those will be some of the ways potential buyers will look for you. You can also use the free Overture Suggestion Tool at http://inventory.overture.com/d/searchinventory/suggestion/ or the Wordtracker Keyword Research Tool (free trial) at www.wordtracker.com to broaden your search for targeted keywords.

Reviews and Guides

The Reviews and Guides section found on eBay's home page is a clever marketing tool that sellers can use to gain more exposure, while offering reviews, critiques, and advice to interested parties on a variety of topics. Under Reviews, members are encouraged to post their personal reviews about movies, books, music, games, electronic equipment, and other products. This helps shoppers know whether or not the item is worth investing in. In the Guides section, members can offer advice on any topic or category. For example, if you are a cooking aficionado, you can share favorite recipes or baking tips with viewers. Perhaps you've had a positive experience on eBay that would benefit other users. In both sections, your User ID, Store, and About Me page will be prominently displayed and readers can vote on whether or not they found the information you posted to be helpful, while checking out your auctions or store.

Word-of-Mouth

Word-of-mouth is the most powerful form of marketing. Don't be shy about asking your family, friends, associates and off-eBay customers to check out your auctions and visit your eBay store. You should also ask them to spread the word to their friends—if you're offering quality merchandise, they'll be happy to help.

Special Purchases

Special purchases can be a marketing tool. When you find a super deal on a great product, let your existing customers know what you've got, and tell them they need to buy now to take advantage of this special price.

Rules about Advertising

Online advertisements—and your eBay auctions are advertisements—are subject to the same rules that apply to other forms of advertising. In short, advertising must tell the truth and not mislead consumers, and claims must be substantiated.

One of the key missions of the FTC is to prevent deceptive and unfair acts or practices. According to the FTC, a representation, omission, or practice is deceptive if it is likely to mislead consumers and affect consumers' behavior or decisions about the product or service. An act or practice is unfair if the injury it causes or is likely to cause is substantial, not outweighed by other benefits and not reasonably avoidable. Federal law prohibits unfair or deceptive advertising in any medium.

If you are selling goods you obtain from a manufacturer or distributor, ask for material to back up claims before you repeat what the manufacturer says about the product in your listing. If the manufacturer fails to provide the proof or gives you something that looks questionable, be very cautious about proceeding. Trust your instincts, and if the claims sound too good to be true, they probably are. And remember that all disclaimers and disclosures must be clear and conspicuous.

If your advertisements fail to comply with the law, you could face enforcement actions or civil lawsuits. That could mean orders to cease and desist, with fines up to $11,000 per violation; injunctions by federal district courts; and in some instances, refunds to consumers for actual damages in civil lawsuits.

Publicity and Public Relations

To gain the benefits of publicity and public relations, you must first understand what they are and why they're important to your business. A very simple way to explain publicity is that it is the process of getting yourself, your company, or your product mentioned in a print or broadcast story. You do this by suggesting to journalists—usually in the form of a news release, but you could also do it over the phone or via e-mail—that there is something about your organization that is newsworthy or otherwise of strong enough interest to be featured. You do not pay for this coverage, nor do you have any control over what journalists ultimately say in their coverage. This is in stark contrast to advertising, where you buy the space and control exactly what goes in it.

Public relations includes publicity, but it is a broader issue that encompasses such efforts as public image, investor relations, crisis communications, special events and sponsorships, and other activities that have an influence on how the public perceives you and your company.

By virtue of its tremendous size and market, eBay as a company is routinely covered in the business media. That's good for all eBay sellers because it attracts new users, and therefore more potential customers for you.

But the publicity that will be of most value to you is the publicity you generate yourself. When you do something that's newsworthy, issue a release to your local media outlets. If the business section of your local paper includes new business announcements, be sure yours gets in there. When you add a product line, expand your services, reach a certain sales goal, or hire new people, issue a news release.

When something happens on a national level that relates to what you do or the types of merchandise you sell, write up a media advisory with a local spin. Local reporters love to be able to interview someone in their own community. You can send a note (either fax or e-mail) to the local paper and radio and television stations repeating the news story and offering to answer additional questions.

When you see print or broadcast stories on people who are selling interesting or unusual items on eBay, those pieces are usually prompted by the eBay users, not eBay's corporate public relations department. The mission of eBay's PR staff is to deal with corporate public relations, and they do not have the resources to help promote individual auctions or sellers. Typically, eBay sellers are the ones who generate media attention because reporters are more interested in covering a story about an item on eBay if that overture comes from the seller and not from a paid PR person on eBay's payroll. Also, sellers are likely to be more familiar with their specific media outlets, such as local and industry publications.

Trade Shows

Regardless of what type of items you sell on eBay, you may benefit from attending and possibly even exhibiting in trade shows. Shows provide a venue for you to find merchandise that you can sell on eBay, make contacts with wholesalers and other business product and service providers, learn more about running your business, and market your own products. Local trade shows can provide a tremendous amount of exposure at a very affordable cost and can be a great networking opportunity.

There are two types of shows—consumer (which focus on home, garden, and other consumer themes) and business-to-business (where exhibitors market their products and services to other companies).

"When you go to a show, you're tapping into an audience that is typically outside your network," says trade show consultant Allen Konopacki. "The other important thing is that the individuals who are going to shows are usually driven by a need. In fact, 76 percent of the people who go to a show are looking to make some kind of a decision on a purchase in the near future."

Tip...

Smart Tip

Trade shows and conventions are valuable business tools, whether you're attending to shop and learn or exhibiting to get more business. For information on how to get more out of trade shows and to find show schedules, visit these trade show web sites: Incomm Research Center, www.tradeshow research.com; Trade Show News Network, www.tsnn.com; and Tradeshow Week On-Line, www.tradeshowweek.com.

A show is an opportunity to let prospective customers see your merchandise on display so they'll feel more comfortable bidding on your auctions or shopping in your eBay store. Of course, if they buy at the show, all the better.

To find out about local shows in your area, call your local chamber of commerce or convention center and ask for a calendar. You can also check out *Tradeshow Week Show Directory* (Reed Business Information), which should be available in your public library, or do an internet search.

On with the Trade Show

A carnival-like atmosphere permeates many trade shows. Of course, you want everyone involved to enjoy themselves, but remember, this is a business occasion. Your booth is your store/office for the duration of the show, and it should be a place where you are proud to meet with customers. Establishing dress and conduct rules for your booth ahead of time will make your trade show experience much more rewarding. Abide by these rules:

○ *No smoking, drinking, eating, or gum-chewing by booth staffers.* Too many people are offended by cigarette smoke, and most exhibit halls restrict smoking to designated areas anyway. While most shows provide refreshments, bringing food and beverages into the booth creates an unattractive mess. Who wants to talk to a sales rep whose mouth is full of Cheetos?

○ *Dress appropriately.* Just because the show takes place in a resort doesn't mean you should wear shorts and a tank top. Standard business attire and comfortable shoes are your best bet.

○ *Staff the booth properly.* Two people for every 10 feet of space is a good rule of thumb. The key is to make sure your booth is not overcrowded with your own people, or so understaffed that visitors can't get the assistance they need.

○ *Take regular breaks.* Trade shows can be exhausting. Plan to allow everyone a few minutes away from the booth at scheduled intervals. Also allow time for personnel to see the entire show as early as possible; they'll gain a feel for the competition and pick up ideas for your next show.

○ *Remain standing and talk to each other only when necessary.* Visitors may be reluctant to approach your booth if it appears your salespeople are just relaxing and having a great time chatting among themselves.

When you have identified potential shows, contact the sponsor for details. Find out who will attend—show sponsors should be able to estimate the total number and give you demographics so you can tell if the attendees fit your target-market profile. Also ask if it's appropriate to make sales from your booth so you can plan your display and bring sufficient inventory.

Give as much thought to the setup of your booth as you would to an in-store display. Your exhibit does not need to be elaborate or expensive, but it does need to be professional and inviting. Avoid trying to cram so much into your booth that it looks cluttered. Your signage should focus first on the problems you solve for clients and then list your company name. Even though the show sponsors will probably provide

▲

one, do not put a table across the front of your exhibit space; that creates a visual and psychological barrier and will discourage visitors from coming in.

Don't leave your booth unattended during exhibit hours. First, it's a security risk—at a busy show, it would be easy for someone to walk off with valuable merchandise. But more important, you could miss a tremendous sales opportunity. Even if you're a one-person operation, find someone who can work the show with you so that you can take breaks during the day.

Consider some sort of giveaway item such as pens, mugs, or notepads imprinted with your company name. But, says Konopacki, do not display these items openly; that will only crowd your booth with "trade show tourists." Instead, store them discreetly out of sight, and present them individually as appropriate. You should also have a stock of brochures, business cards, and perhaps discount coupons.

To collect lead information for later follow-up, consider holding a drawing that people must register for, and make the registration form a lead-qualification tool that asks for information so you can follow up with a sales call later. When the show is over, immediately send a letter to all the qualified leads you collected, thanking them for visiting your booth and reminding them of the products and services you offer. Don't assume that they'll keep the information they picked up at the show; chances are, it will be lost in the pile of material they received from other exhibitors.

15

Staffing Your Company

Plenty of eBay sellers make comfortable incomes as solo operators, handling everything themselves. They deliberately keep their companies as one-person operations because they don't want to deal with the headaches that growth can bring. They're happy that way and have no desire to do anything different. While there's nothing wrong with this strategy, if your goal is growth, you will reach a point where you must hire people. And even if your goal isn't growth, there may be times when you need help, so it's important to understand the basics of finding, hiring, and managing personnel.

You may find it difficult to turn over tasks to someone else, especially if you've never supervised or managed people before. There's little anyone else can tell you to make this leap easier; you just have to do it—and believe that it will be worth the effort. As your business grows, don't make the mistake of trying to do too much yourself and not hiring customer service staffers soon enough.

Let's consider the process of adding staff to your operation. The first step is to decide exactly what you want someone to do and write a job description. The job description you write doesn't have to be as formal as one you might expect from a large corporation, but it needs to clearly outline the person's duties and responsibilities. It should also list any special skills or other required credentials, such as a valid driver's license and clean driving record for someone who is going to take packages to the post office and run other errands for you, or computer skills for administrative help.

Next, you need to establish a pay scale. This will depend on what you are hiring people to do, the skills needed, and the pay scales in your area. All the eBay sellers we talked to who had employees say they pay their staff competitively based on their job descriptions and the market.

You should also have a job application form. No matter which one you choose, have your attorney review the form you will be using for compliance with the most current employment laws.

Every prospective employee should fill out an application—even if it's someone you already know, and even if they've submitted a detailed resume. A resume is not a signed, sworn statement acknowledging that you can fire them if they lie; the application is. The application will also help you verify their resumes; compare the two and make sure the information is consistent.

Now you're ready to start looking for candidates.

Looking for Employees in All the Right Places

Picture the ideal candidate in your mind. Is this person likely to be unemployed and reading the classified ads? It's possible, but you will probably improve your chances for a successful hire if you're more creative in your search techniques than simply writing a "help wanted" ad.

Network with personal and professional associates to identify prospective employees—you never know who might know the perfect person for your company. Check with nearby colleges and perhaps even high schools for part-time help.

Another option is to use a temporary help or employment agency. Many small businesses shy away from agencies because they feel like they can't afford the fee—but if the agency handles the advertising, initial screening, and background checks, their fee may be well worth paying.

Use caution if you decide to hire friends and relatives—many personal relationships have not been strong enough to survive an employee-employer situation. Small-business owners tell of nightmarish experiences when a friend or relative refused to accept direction or in other ways abused a personal relationship in the course of business. Jonathan Garriss, whose partner in their eBay business, Gotham City Online, is a friend, notes that small-business owners tend to hire people they know. "One of the challenges when you hire someone you know is that it's tough to separate business from friendship, and eventually the relationship changes," he says. He adds it's critical to establish boundaries from the start. "Make sure both parties understand that this is a business relationship, and in the office you are boss and employee."

> **Tip...**
>
> **Smart Tip**
> Consider how you can tie compensation to performance so workers have a clear incentive to do a great job.

Evaluating Applicants

What kinds of people make good employees for a company that sells on eBay? It depends on what you want them to do. If you're hiring someone as a driver, that person should have a good driving record and know the city. If you're hiring someone to help with administrative tasks, they need to have computer know-how and be able to learn your operating system. If you're hiring someone to handle customer service, they need to know your products and policies, care about people, and be able to react quickly and calmly to surprises. What is really important is that the people you hire are committed to giving you their best effort during the time they're working so that your customers receive the best service.

Garriss of Gotham City Online has about 30 employees, most of them full time. He says that everyone who works for him, from office staff to warehouse workers, is comfortable with technology and knows about clothing. "Everyone is using technology here," he says. "But they're not a bunch of techies. They know clothing, they know fashion, and they know their jobs. The way we have integrated technology makes their jobs easier."

When you actually begin the hiring process, don't be surprised if you're as nervous at the prospect of interviewing potential employees as they are about being interviewed. After all, they may need a job—but the future of your company is at stake.

It's a good idea to prepare your interview questions in advance. Develop open-ended questions that encourage the candidate to talk. In addition to knowing what they've done, you want to find out how they did it. Ask each candidate the same set of questions, and make notes as they respond so you can make an accurate assessment and comparison later.

When the interview is over, let the candidate know what to expect. Is it going to take you several weeks to interview other candidates, check references, and make a decision? Will you want the top candidates to return for a second interview? Will you call the candidates, or should they call you? This is not only a good business practice, it's also simple common courtesy.

Always check the former employers and personal references of your candidates. Though many companies are very restrictive as to what information they'll verify, you may be surprised at what you can find out. You should at least confirm that the applicant told the truth about dates and positions held. Personal references are likely to give you some additional insight into the general character and personality of the candidate; this will help you decide if they'll be a match for your culture and fit into your operation.

Be sure to document every step of the interview and reference-checking process. Even very small companies are finding themselves the targets of employment discrimination suits; good records are your best defense if it happens to you.

Once They're on Board

The hiring process is only the beginning of the challenge of having employees. The next thing you need to do is train them.

Many small businesses conduct their "training" just by throwing someone into the job, but that's not fair to the employee, and it's certainly not good for your business. If you think you can't afford to spend time on training, think again—can you afford not to adequately train your employees? Do you really want them interacting with your customers when you haven't told them how you want things done?

In an ideal world, employees could be hired already knowing everything they need to know. But this isn't an ideal world, and if you want the job done right, you have to teach your people how to do it.

Whether done in a formal classroom setting or on the job, effective training begins with a clear goal and a plan for reaching it. Training will fall into one of three major categories: orientation, which includes explaining company policies and procedures; job skills, which focuses on how to do specific tasks; and ongoing development, which enhances the basic job skills and grooms employees for future challenges and opportunities. Heed the following tips; doing so will help maximize your training efforts:

> **Tip...**
>
> **Smart Tip**
>
> Training employees—even part-time, temporary help—to understand your way of doing things is extremely important. These people are representing your company, and they need to maintain the image and standards you have worked hard to establish.

- *Find out how people learn best.* Training employees is not a one-size-fits-all proposition. People absorb and process information differently, so your training method needs to be compatible with their individual preferences. Some people can read a manual, others prefer a verbal explanation, and still others need to see a demonstration. In a group-training situation, your best strategy is to use a combination of methods; when you're working one-on-one, tailor your delivery to fit the needs of the person you're training. With some employees, figuring out how they learn best can be a simple matter of asking them. Others may not know what their preferred learning style is. In those cases, experiment with various training styles and see what works best for the specific employee.

You Deserve a Break Today

No matter how much you enjoy your work, you need an occasional break from it. This is a particular challenge for solo operators, but it's critical. You need to be away from your operation occasionally, not only for vacations but also for business reasons, such as attending conferences and trade shows. Also, you need a plan in place in case of illness, an accident, or other emergencies.

It's also important to take regular time-outs for yourself so that that you are not overloaded. Jonathan Garriss of Gotham City Online points out that as hard as he works, he knows how important it is to "take a little bit of time off and decompress."

If you're a one- or two-person operation, with proper planning you should be able to take a long weekend or just one or two days off without your customers even knowing you're gone. For longer periods away, you need to find someone you can trust who will run the business for you in your absence. With a staff to depend on, taking a vacation is easier—just be sure your people are well-trained and committed to maintaining your service levels when you aren't there.

Try these vacation-planning tips on for size:

- *Plan ahead.* Schedule your vacation time far enough in advance that you can plan your workload around your time off. For example, you can stop listing auctions while you're gone.
- *Build a backup network.* Look for people you trust who can handle work that can't wait while you're gone, such as orders from your eBay store or web site.
- *Notify your regular customers.* About two weeks before you leave, tell the customers with whom you communicate regularly that you'll be unavailable so they can place any upcoming orders before you go.

▲

- *Use simulation and role-playing to train, practice, and reinforce.* One of the most effective training techniques is simulation, which involves showing an employee how to do something, and then allowing them to practice it in a safe, controlled environment.

- *Be a strong role model.* Don't expect more from your employees than you expect from yourself. You're a good role model when you do things the way they should be done all the time. Don't take shortcuts you don't want your employees to take, and don't behave in any way that you don't want them to behave. On the other hand, don't assume that simply doing things the right way is enough to teach others how to do things. Role-modeling is not a substitute for training—it reinforces training. If you only act as a role model but never train others to be one, employees aren't likely to get the message.

- *Look for training opportunities.* Once you get beyond basic orientation and job-skills training, you need to constantly be on the lookout for opportunities to enhance the skills and performance levels of your people.

- *Make it real.* Whenever possible, use real-life situations to train. For example, you might want to let a new customer service rep draft responses to bidder e-mails, but you or another experienced worker should review them before they're sent. If you do this, be sure to avoid letting customers know they've become a training experience for employees.

- *Anticipate questions.* Don't assume employees know what to ask. In a new situation, people often don't understand enough to ask questions. Anticipate their questions, and answer them in advance.

- *Ask for feedback.* Just as your eBay customers let you know what they thought of their transaction with you, encourage employees to tell you how you're doing as a trainer. Explain that you'll evaluate their performance, so it's OK for them to tell you the truth; ask them what they thought of the training and your techniques, and use that information to improve your own skills.

Employee Benefits

The actual wages you pay may be only part of your employees' total compensation. While many very small companies do not offer a formal benefits program, more and more business owners have recognized that benefits—particularly in the area of insurance—are extremely important when it comes to attracting and retaining quality employees. Regardless of the overall employment situation, competition for good people is stiff almost everywhere.

Typical benefit packages include group insurance (your employees may pay all or a portion of their premiums), paid holidays and vacations. You can build employee loy-

Bright Idea

Look for special, unexpected ways to reward your employees for a job well done. Take them to lunch, give them gift certificates or tickets for recreational events, or simply recognize them in front of other employees.

alty by seeking additional benefits that may be somewhat unusual—and they don't have to cost much. For example, if you're in a retail location, talk to other store owners in your shopping center to see if they're interested in providing reciprocal employee discounts. You'll not only provide your own employees with a benefit, but you may get some new customers out of the arrangement.

Gotham City Online offers health insurance and is working on developing a 401(k) plan. Garriss says he is always looking for ways to enhance the company's benefits package. Boston Tables' Andrew Robinson says his company's benefits package includes medical and dental insurance.

Short-Term Solutions

Wholesale manufacturer and import distributor David Lynn has a college intern and two full-time customer service reps who stay consistently busy on the eBay side of the business. But his need for help in the warehouse fluctuates from week to week depending on how many containers CRI receives and how much additional labor is needed to help unload trucks when they arrive. On some days, Lynn and his regular staff can handle the routine shipping and inventory tasks. So rather than hire full-time workers for a job that's not full time, he uses a temporary labor service. Though his

Cover Me

In most states, if you have three or more employees, you are required by law to carry workers' compensation insurance. This coverage pays medical expenses and replaces a portion of the employee's wages if he or she is injured on the job. Even if you have only one or two employees, you may want to consider obtaining this coverage to protect both them and you in the event of an accident.

Details and requirements vary by state; contact your state's insurance office or your own insurance agent for information so you can be sure you're in compliance.

▲

actual hourly rate is higher than it would be if these were his employees, the overall savings in both cash and efficiency makes it worth it to him.

You may also find that certain tasks can be handled by an independent contractor or consultant. Consider outsourcing work in the areas of accounting and record-keeping, special marketing projects, etc. If you have tasks you need help with but that don't fit the parameters of a regular part- or full-time position, look for nontraditional ways to get them done.

Tales from the Trenches

By now you should know how to get started and have a good idea of what to do—and what not to do—when you're selling on eBay. But nothing teaches as well as the voice of experience. So we asked established eBay sellers to tell us what has contributed to their success and what they think causes companies that don't make it to fail. Here's what they said:

Beware!

Think before you speak! Long Beach, California, eBay entrepreneur Buz Moran says one of the dangers of being a successful eBay seller is that when you visit your friends' homes, you'll constantly be picking up items and saying, "Do you know what you could get for this on eBay?"

Consider Advice Carefully

As soon as you go into business for yourself, you'll be deluged with well-meaning advice. Jonathan Garriss of Gotham City Online says, "We got so much advice from people, and, unfortunately, three-fourths of it was wrong. What paid off for us was to take a common-sense approach. Ask yourself 'Does this make sense?' "

He says it's important to first understand what you're doing, and then you can evaluate how advice from someone else will fit into your operation. "If there is something you don't understand or doesn't make sense to you, think twice," he recommends. He says you'll often get advice from people who are working through business models that are decades old, using techniques that may have been cutting-edge 20 years ago, but that just won't work today.

A Sustainable Plan

eBay is full of stories—and, in fact, we've told some of them in this book—of people who pick up something for pennies and sell it for hundreds of dollars on eBay. "Those are great isolated success stories," says Garriss. "But if you're looking to build a business based on buying things for $1 and selling them for $1,000, that is not a sustainable business model."

It's important, he says, to have realistic expectations. "People think eBay is like the great California Gold Rush," he says. "But it's work. You need to have knowledge of the marketplace and an understanding of what your business is going to be."

Consultant Paul Mladjenovic says one of the biggest mistakes new eBay sellers make is "thinking that they are going to make a fortune with one listing, when they should be doing multiple listings, tweaking, learning, analyzing, upgrading, modifying, and understanding their market as they go along."

Part-time Oviedo, Florida, eBay seller Liz Baker agrees: "People think they can buy a really cheap product and make a lot of money with not a lot of work. It just doesn't happen that way."

Though he's been lucky on eBay, Long Beach, California, eBay entrepreneur Buz Moran says, "I'm not trying to hit a home run every time. I'm just trying to turn my dime into a dollar."

Keep the Cash Flowing

Don't worry if you take a loss on an item every now and then. Understand what happened (usually it's because you paid more than you should have), and keep going. You need to maintain a steady cash flow if you're going to be in a position to take advantage of opportunities when they arise, so keep buying and selling, buying and selling.

Don't Charge Until You Ship

If you have your own credit card merchant account, get a preauthorization for the amount of the sale, but don't actually charge your customer's account until you have shipped the merchandise. If something happens and you are unable to ship immediately, customers are inclined to be far more forgiving if you haven't charged them for the merchandise they haven't received. For example, if you encounter problems getting your inventory delivered or the items shipped due to a transportation strike or some other reason beyond your control, you customers are less likely to be angry if they haven't been charged. They may not be happy about the delay, but they will probably be a lot more understanding if they haven't paid for something they don't have in their hands.

Get Rid of Items That Don't Sell

It happens to every retailer at one time or another: You invest in inventory you thought would sell, but it doesn't. So what do you do with it? If you bought it from a wholesaler with a return policy, consider taking advantage of that. But in most cases, you'll need to dump that unsold inventory in some way.

Some ideas from successful eBay sellers are:

- *Batch like items together, and sell them as a lot on eBay.* "Instead of selling the items one at a time, lump them together and sell them all at once," antiques seller Sue Rudolph advises. "I had some antique Christmas ornaments that I tried to sell singly a couple of years in a row, but the reserves weren't met. So I put them all together in a group, and they sold for more than the total of what I wanted for them individually."

- *For multiple items that are identical, drop the price, and list them in a Dutch auction.* For example, if you have items that have been in your inventory for several months but haven't moved very well, try putting four or five up at a time, and they may sell more quickly.

- *Reduce your starting bid and relist.* It's a fact of life in retailing: Sometimes you have to sell things at a loss to turn your inventory. "My inventory is small enough that I know if something has been around and unsold long enough, it's

▲

about to start costing me," says Liz Baker. "I'll sell those items at or below cost because I need my money back to buy more things."

Rudolph agrees: "Sometimes you have to dump stuff. You might end up taking a loss, but at least you've gotten rid of it."

- *Hold a garage sale.* Moran says that once or twice a year he holds his own garage sale to clear out eBay inventory that isn't selling.

> ⚠️ **Beware!**
> Walk before you run. When you first start listing items, don't put up 100 auctions at once. Just do a couple at a time until you are used to keeping track of things.

- *Give it to charity, and take a tax deduction.* Gotham City Online's consignment agreement allows the company to donate merchandise that doesn't sell to charities. Similarly, Laurie Ayers often buys from thrift stores, so when something doesn't sell, she donates back to the store where she bought it so that they can sell it again.

The Bottom Line

Is selling on eBay for you? Perhaps. Only you can make that call. For those who are cut out for this type of business, the bottom line is that eBay is a fun and potentially profitable place to do business, whether your goal is to generate occasional part-time income working by yourself from home or to build a substantial operation with commercial facilities and employees—or something in between. So if this sounds like your cup of tea, decide what you're going to sell, get out your camera, write your description, and go!

Appendix

eBay Business Resources

They say you can never be too rich or too thin. While these could be argued, we believe "You can never have too many resources." Therefore, we present for your consideration a wealth of sources for you to check into, check out, and harness for your own personal information blitz.

These sources are tidbits, ideas to get you started on your research. They are by no means the only sources out there, and they should not be taken as the Ultimate Answer. We have done our research, but businesses—like customers—tend to move, change, fold, and expand. As we have repeatedly stressed, do your homework. Get out and start investigating.

Associations and Organizations

Disabled Online Users Association (DOUA), a network of individuals who are learning and teaching how to earn a living by selling on the internet, www.doua.org

National Mail Order Association LLC, (612) 788-1673, www.nmoa.org

Online Traders Web Alliance (OTWA), an online auction association dedicated to the independent online auction seller and merchant, www.otwa.com

The Auction Guild Inc. (TAG), (877) SAFETAG, www.theauctionguild.com

Auction Software and Support

Andale Inc., online auction management products and services, (866) 220-5099 or (650) 230-3000, www.andale.com

Auction Hawk, eBay auction management products, www.auctionhawk.com

AuctionHelper Inc., auction management tools for online auctions, www.auctionhelper.com

Auction Moms, a resource for beginners, with free templates, tools, and tips, www.auctionmoms.com

Auction Patrol, forums, tools, directory, picture, and auction management, www.auctionpatrol.com

Auction Watch, online auction management products and services, (650) 808-5800, www.auctionwatch.com

Auction Wizard 2000, auction management software, www.auctionwizard2000.com

Auctionworks Inc., online auction software and services, (877) 668-2655, www.auctionworks.com

Auctiva Corp., auction management tools, (530) 892-9191, www.auctiva.com

ChannelAdvisor Corp., auction management tools, (866) 264-8594, www.channeladvisor.com

Infopia Inc., comprehensive e-commerce solution with tight eBay integration, (888) 337-6352, www.infopia.com

ManageAuctions.com, online auction management services, www.manageauctions.com

Marketworks Inc., full-featured suite of auction listing services, (800) 406-9260, www.marketworks.com

MyAuctionMate, auction management software, www.myauctionmate.com

Nucite, auction templates (some free) and other services, www.nucite.com

Pics Plus Image Hosting, image hosting, www.pics-plus.com

SpareDollar Inc., auction management services, www.sparedollar.com

Vendio Services Inc., comprehensive auction sales manager, (650) 808-5800, www.vendio.com

Zoovy Inc., auction management and e-commerce software, (877) 966-8948, www.zoovy.com

Consultants and Other Experts

Allen Konopacki, Ph.D., trade show consultant, Incomm Research Center, (312) 642-9377, www.tradeshowresearch.com

David Lynn, Combined Resources International, e-mail: ebay@cri2000.com, eBay user ID: combined_direct, www.cri2000.com

Paul Mladjenovic, consultant and small-business specialist and teaches classes on internet auctions: Prosperity Network, (201) 714-4953, www.mladjenovic.com, www.superauctionlinks.com

Chuck Norman, CPA, Partner, Ernst & Young, (419) 321-5470, www.ey.com

Internet Resources

AuctionSnipe, fully automated sniping solution to help win auctions, www.auctionsnipe.com

Big Ideas for Small Businesses, www.bwideas.com

Big Lots!, closeout merchandise, www.biglotswholesale.com

Consumer Product Safety Commission, www.cpsc.gov

Corel Paint Shop Family, help creating professional-looking images, www.jasc.com

eSnipe, online service (not software) that bids for you at the last second, www.esnipe.com

Federal Trade Commission, www.ftc.gov

Flea Market Guide, comprehensive listing of U.S. flea markets, http://fleamarketguide.com

Free Misspelled Words Toolbar, www.misspellsearch.com

Gatorpack Shipping Supplies, (888) 258-8555, e-mail: gatorpacksells@aol.com, www.gatorpack.com

Internet Auction List, www.internetauctionlist.com

Picasa Picture Simplicity, software that helps you find, edit, and share all the pictures on your PC, http://picasa.google.com/index.html

Sam's Club, closeout deals, http://auctions.samsclub.com

Smart Shipping, a variety of shipping resources, including carriers, supplies, and services, www.smartshipping.com

Stamps.com, internet postage, www.stamps.com

Tax Saving Educational Tools, http://taxloopholes.com

Tuesday Morning, brand-name closeout store, www.tuesdaymorning.com

Two Pilots, photo-enhancing software, www.colorpilot.com,

U.S. Business Advisor, www.business.gov

U.S. Treasury, seized property auctions, www.ustreas.gov/auctions

What Do I Sell, www.whatdoisell.com

Worldwide Brands, www.worldwidebrands.com

Payment Resources

Authorize.Net Corp., (801) 492-6450, www.authorizenet.com

CCNow, (877) 226-6977, www.ccnow.com

E-Gold, (321) 956-1200, www.e-gold.com

Escrow.com, (714) 751-6290, www.escrow.com

Glo-Bill, (888) 746-4217, www.globill-systems.com

Internet Billing Co. Ltd., (888) 371-7800, www.ibill.com

Paying Fast, www.payingfast.com

PayPal, www.paypal.com

PaySystems.com Inc., (514) 227-6868, www.paysystems.com

Western Union BidPay, BidPay.com Inc., www.bidpay.com

WorldPay Inc., (703) 444-0260, www.worldpay.com

Publications

eBay for Dummies, Marsha Collier, Hungry Minds

eBay Smart: Building a Real eBay Business by Going Beyond the Get-Rich-Quick Game (CD-ROM), Kevin S. Peterson, SpinSmart Software

Make BIG Profits on eBay: Start Your Own Million $ Business, Jacquelyn Lynn and Charlene Davis, Entrepreneur Press

Starting an eBay Business for Dummies, Marsha Collier, Hungry Minds

Starting Your Online Auction Business, Denis L. Prince, Prima Tech

The Official eBay Bible, Jim "Griff" Griffith, Gotham

Shipping Companies

DHL, www.dhl-usa.com

FedEx, www.fedex.com

United Parcel Service, www.ups.com

United States Postal Service, www.usps.com

Successful eBay Sellers

Laurie Ayers, Granville, MI, www.laurieayers.com, eBay user ID: taekwondough

Liz Baker, Oviedo, FL, www.busymomsrecipes.com, e-mail: ebay@busymomsrecipes.com, eBay user ID: theliteratelady

Jonathan Garriss, Gotham City Online, (201) 330-9093, www.gothamcityonline.com, eBay user ID: gothamcityonline

Georgene Harkness, My New Threads, Plano, TX, www.mynewthreads.com, www.hostpci.com, eBay user ID: mynewthreads

Gary and Susan Marler, Selma, NC, Gary's e-mail: royaluph@nc.rr.com, Susan's e-mail: smarler514@nc.rr.com, Gary's eBay user ID: wizard5482, Susan's eBay user ID: ozfreak2

Buz Moran, Long Beach, CA, e-mail: jewel777@worldnet.att.net, eBay user ID: chubbychums

Andrew Robinson, Boston Tables, (614) 337-7665, www.bostontables.com, eBay user ID: bostontables

Sue Rudolph, Sweet Sue's Antiques and Appraisals, Winter Park, FL, e-mail: suru@worldnet.att.net, eBay user ID: suru2

Peggy Webb, Pages-and-More, Sisters, OR, http://stores.ebay.com/Pages-and-More, eBay user ID: wwwebbs

Bob Willey, Bob's Neat Stuff, (410) 228-9211 Office, e-mail: bobwilley@bobsstuff.com, eBay user ID: bobwilley, http://BobsStuff.com, http://BobsNeatStuff.com, http://LetMeSellOnEbay.com, http://LetMeSellFoundValue.com

Glossary

About Me: an eBay page that tells other users about you, your merchandise, and your selling terms and conditions

Acquiring bank: in online payment processing, this is the bank that provides internet merchant accounts

Ad format listings: advertisements for products and services on eBay, as opposed to auctions

Add-on selling: encouraging customers to buy additional, related items; also referred to as suggestive selling and companion selling

Advanced search: a detailed search that allows you to find specific eBay users, look for items using different keyword strategies, and search completed listings

Announcements Board: a special online bulletin board where eBay posts timely information and updates; regular eBay users should check this board daily

Auction management software: software that allows sellers to monitor auctions and perform listing activities in one place

Auction-style listing: a traditional auction where a seller lists one or more items with a starting price; buyers are able to bid on the auction until it ends with the highest bidder winning

Authorization: the process of verifying that a customer's credit card is active and that the customer has sufficient available credit to complete the transaction; for online payments, the authorization process also verifies the customer's billing information

Auto sig: an automatic signature attached to your outgoing e-mail

Best Offer: allows buyers to suggest a price they are willing to pay for an item; this is a free feature but must be used in conjunction with Buy It Now

Bid: a buyer enters the maximum amount he or she is willing to pay for an item, which is increased incrementally; considered binding unless retracted or cancelled

Bid cancellation: the cancellation of a bid by a buyer or seller

Bid increment: the amount by which a bid is increased each time the current bid is outdone

Bid retraction: the withdrawal of a bid; bid retractions are rarely allowed on eBay

Bid shielding: using secondary user IDs or other eBay members to temporarily raise bidding to extremely high levels to protect the low bid level of another bidder; when bid shielding, the high bidder retracts the bid before the auction closes

Bidder search: a search for all the items on which a particular user has placed bids

Bidding: the act of placing a bid on an auction item

Bill of lading (BOL): the mandatory paperwork necessary when shipping by common carrier that includes all the details needed to process and bill the shipment

Buy It Now (BIN): a feature that allows buyers to purchase an item for a fixed price, bypassing the bidding process; can be used in auction-style or fixedprice listings

C.O.D. (cash on delivery): payment at the time the merchandise is delivered or picked up by the customer

Card not present: a term used by credit card companies to describe a transaction when the seller has not seen the actual credit card; typically, this applies to internet and mail order sales

Certified Provider: a technical or nontechnical solution provider offering third-party services to eBay users after meeting specific criteria and compliance standards established by eBay

Community: a term used to identify eBay members, including buyers and sellers, who can also chat on discussion forums, boards, and groups

Completed item search: a search of eBay auctions that have ended

Customer issuing bank: a financial institution that provides a customer with a credit card or other payment instrument

Cybercrime: crime related to technology, computers, and the internet

Dimensional weight: a standard formula used in the freight industry that considers a package's density when determining charges; charges are based on the actual weight or the dimensional weight, whichever is greater

Discount: the amount by which a price is reduced to create an incentive for various consumer behaviors, such as to increase sales or encourage early payment

Discussion board: an area within the eBay Community where members can discuss eBay-related topics

Domain name: the textual name assigned to a host on the internet

Drop-shipping: when a seller uses a wholesaler to ship auction items to winning bidders

Dutch auction: when a seller has two or more identical items offered in the same auction; also known as a multiple item auction

Dutch avoidance: avoiding posting a Dutch auction by listing a single item and offering additional items for sale in the item description; this is a violation of eBay policy

eBay Live auctions: a way to bid real-time at offline auctions through eBay

eBay Motors: a special section in eBay that auctions cars, trucks, and motorcycles, as well as parts and accessories for motor vehicles

eBay shipping calculator: a tool sellers can insert in auction descriptions that allows buyers to determine how much shipping will cost to their ZIP code

eBay stores: a venue for sellers to promote inventory through fixed price listings

eBay toolbar: a free downloadable tool for your web browser that provides easy access to auction listings, as well as additional security for your account

Featured listing: a marketing service provided by eBay that gives auctions extra exposure in the "Featured" sections at the top of listings pages

Feedback: comments made by one user about another regarding the trading experience between the two parties

Final value: the final bid on an auction; the amount for which the item sells

Final value fee: the percentage of the final value that is paid by the seller to eBay as part of the listing fees

Fixed price listing: an auction that has a predetermined price on one or more items; there is no bidding and works the same way as the Buy It Now feature

Flat shipping rate: a set shipping rate that a seller charges for an item no matter where the buyer lives

Foot traffic: in retailing, the people walking by or in a store

Gallery picture: for a small fee, sellers can add a thumbnail picture to their auctions that will appear next to the item title in search results

Gift services: an eBay service that allows you to feature your item as a gift and let buyers know that you offer services such as gift wrapping, cards, and shipping directly to the recipient

Gondola: a type of display unit typically used in retail stores, usually a bank of free-standing shelves open on all sides; its primary function is to display goods and provide space for backup stock

Hot item: a designation that appears in search results given to nonreserve items that have received more than 30 bids; hot items are symbolized by a burning match icon

HTML: stands for Hypertext Markup Language, a simple language used to create web pages; this language can be used to enhance eBay listings

ID Verify: establishes proof of identity for sellers and buyers on eBay

Indefinite suspension: the suspension of a user's eBay privileges for more than 60 days with no definite reinstatement date

Insertion fee: the nonrefundable fee charged by eBay to post a listing; insertion fees vary by type of listing

Internet merchant account: a special account with an acquiring bank that allows a merchant to accept credit cards over the internet

Internet service provider (ISP): any company that provides users with access to the internet

Item lookup: a method for searching for an item on eBay when you know the item number

Marking guns: devices used to affix prices or bar codes to retail merchandise

Markup: the amount by which the wholesale price of an item is increased to reach the retail price

Maximum bid: the maximum amount that a buyer is willing to bid and pay for an auction item

Merge: combining several eBay user IDs (including feedback scores and comments) into one

Minimum bid: the lowest amount that can be entered as a bid for a specific auction

Mint: a subjective term used to describe an item that is in perfect condition

Multiple item auction: see Dutch auction

My eBay: a section on eBay that shows all of a member's activity, including sales, purchases, watched items, favorites, account activity, and more

New item: items listed within the preceding 24 hours are considered new and are automatically marked with a rising sun icon, which is removed when the listing is more than 24 hours old

Nonpaying bidder: a bidder who wins an auction but does not pay for the item; eBay has strict policies for dealing with nonpaying bidders

Opening value: another term for starting price or minimum bid

Outbid: a bidder is outbid when another bidder has placed a higher maximum bid than theirs

Outsource: hiring outside firms to provide products and services traditionally handled within a company

Password: a data string used to verify the identity of a user

Payment gateway: a service that provides connectivity among merchants, customers, and financial networks to process and authorize payments

PayPal: eBay's online payment service that allows sellers to accept credit card and bank account payments from buyers

Piracy: the act of illegally copying software, music, or movies that are protected by copyright

PowerSeller: an eBay designation for experienced, reputable eBay sellers who consistently sell a significant volume of items, maintain a 98 percent positive feedback rating, and provide a high level of service; PowerSellers are marked with icons next to their user IDs

Private auction: a type of eBay auction where the bidders' e-mail addresses are not disclosed on the auction page or the bid history page

Processor: a large data center that processes credit card transactions

Prohibited items: items that are not allowed to be sold on eBay

Proxy bidding: a service that allows you to enter the maximum amount you're willing to pay for an item; the eBay system automatically places bids on your behalf, increasing your bid as necessary by the standard increments to maintain your high bid position

Reserve price: a hidden minimum amount the seller is willing to accept for an item listed for auction

Reserve price auction: in a reserve price auction, buyers are not shown the reserve price, and sellers are not obligated to sell if the reserve price is not met

Restricted items: items that have restrictions for selling on eBay but are not necessarily prohibited

RMA: return merchandise authorization; usually a code number issued by a seller who agrees to accept a return

SafeHarbor: the protective arm of eBay that monitors possible misuse of the eBay system and keeps the eBay community safe

Second chance offer: a seller can make an offer to another bidder on an auction item if they have a duplicate, or if the winning bidder fails to pay

Shill bidding: the deliberate placing of bids to artificially raise the price of an item; shill bidding is not allowed on eBay and is illegal in many jurisdictions

Shrinkage: a term used to describe losses when inventory is reduced by theft (either internally or externally) or errors

Signposts: listings that are primarily meant to direct a user to a seller's store or other listings; signposts are not allowed on eBay

Sniping: placing a bid in the closing minutes or seconds of an auction

Spam: unsolicited commercial e-mail

Spoof e-mail or phishing: an e-mail that appears to be from eBay or PayPal asking for personal or financial information (often asking the recipient to verify their eBay or PayPal password); users are advised not to respond to these e-mails and to forward them to either spoof@ebay.com or spoof@paypal.com

Starting price: the price at which bidding on your auction begins; also, the lowest price you are willing to accept unless you have specified a reserve price

Supplier: a company that sells goods and services to other companies

Trademark: any word, name, symbol, or device, or any combination, used or intended to be used in commerce to identify and distinguish the goods of one manufacturer or seller from goods manufactured or sold by others, and to indicate the source of the goods

Trading Assistant: an experienced eBay seller who sells items on eBay for other people on consignment

Trading Post: the physical location (usually a retail store) where a Trading Assistant operates his or her business

Turbo Lister: an eBay tool that allows sellers to create and upload bulk auction listings instead of manually entering information for each auction

Unpaid item: when a buyer commits to buy but does not follow through with payment

User ID: an eBay nickname or screen name chosen by the user

Vendor: another term for supplier

Want It Now: a place on eBay where buyers can post requests for items they are looking for; sellers can respond with matching eBay listings

Index